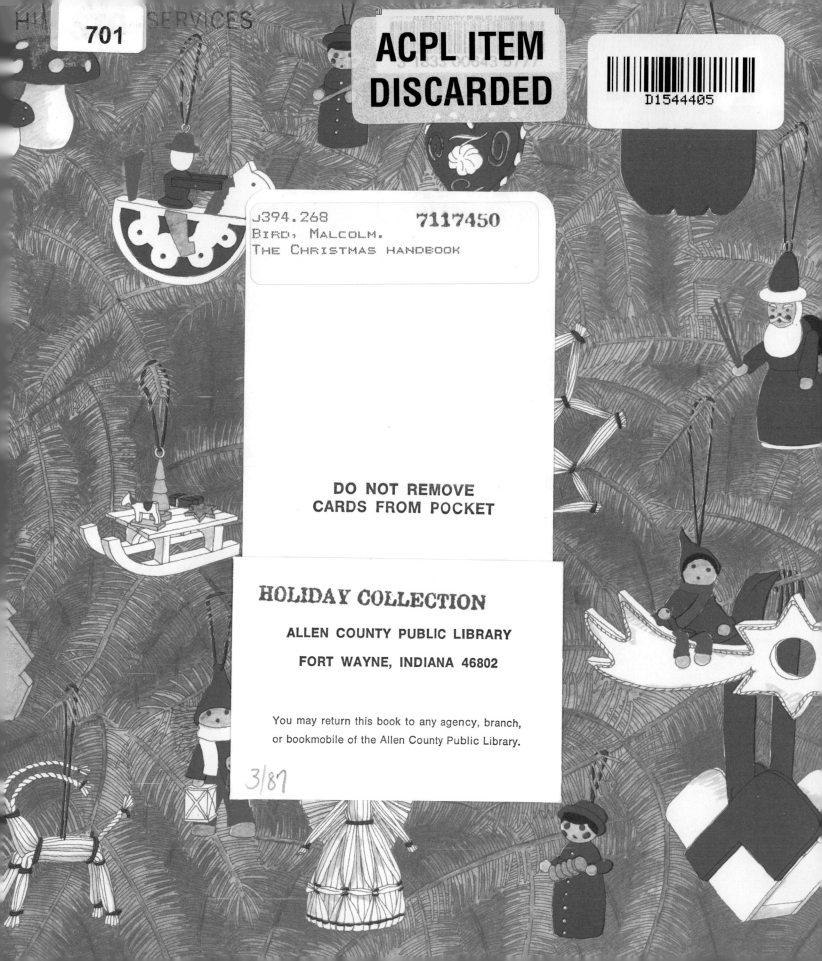

THE CHRISTMAS HANDBOOK

BY
MALCOLM BIRD & ALAN DART

GRANDMA IVY

GRANDPA NICHOLAS

NOEL

CAROL

HOLLY

BABY

ROBIN

JINGLES

THE TINSEL FAMILY

THE CHRISTMAS HANDBOOK

BY
MALCOLM BIRD & ALAN DART

CHILDRENS PRESS CHOICE

A Barron's title selected for educational distribution

ISBN 0-516-08676-6

© Text & ideas – Malcolm Bird and Alan Dart 1986
© Illustrations – Malcolm Bird 1986
First edition for the U.S.A., its territories
and possessions published 1986 by
Barron's Educational Series, Inc.
Library of Congress Catalog CRD Number 86–14051
Produced by David Booth Publishing Ltd,
8 Cranedown, Lewes, East Sussex BN7 3NA England.

FOR MY DEAR PARENTS, PHYL AND JOHN DART. WITH VERY BEST LOVE AND THANKS FOR MAKING EVERY CHRISTMAS SPECIAL. AD

FOR MY PARENTS — EDNA AND GEOFF BIRD, WHO FIRST INTRODUCED ME TO CHRISTMAS. MUCH LOVE AND THANKS FOR ALWAYS ENCOURAGING ME TO DRAW. MB

CONTENTS

7117450

CHAPTER 1

What is Christmas?

What is Christmas?

HERE ARE GRANDMA AND GRANDPA COMING TO STAY FOR CHRISTMAS

MY— YOU'VE ALL GROWN A LOT!

HOW ARE MY THREE FAVORITE GRANDCHILDREN?

WHICH WAY DID YOU DRIVE THIS TIME?

WE'VE FOUND A QUICKER ROUTE— I'LL SHOW YOU ON THE MAP

GRANDMA— WHAT WAS CHRISTMAS LIKE WHEN YOU WERE LITTLE?

I DON'T KNOW IF I CAN REMEMBER THAT LONG AGO!

PLEASE TRY!

I ALWAYS WENT CAROL SINGING WITH MY SCHOOL FRIENDS...

...BUT SOMETIMES I COULDN'T REMEMBER THE WORDS— WASN'T THAT AWFUL?

9

CHAPTER 2

Countdown to Christmas

Advent Crowns

The four weeks leading up to Christmas are called Advent, and start on the Sunday nearest to November 30th. They symbolize the coming of Christ, the fourth week never being completed to signify that His coming will never cease. Advent used to be a period of fasting, but is now more popularly regarded as the countdown to Christmas, when preparations are made for the holidays. A traditional way to celebrate the four Sundays of Advent is to make an Advent crown, a wreath of greenery bearing four candles. On the first Sunday in Advent the first candle on the crown is lit, to be joined by the second candle on the next Sunday, until all four candles are lit on the last Sunday before Christmas. Here we have three variations on the same theme – Candle Wreath is the old-fashioned Advent crown; Glitter Stars is re-usable and represents the Star of Bethlehem, with four smaller stars to add each Sunday; Tinsel Dome bears poster board candles, making it a safe version of the traditional crown.

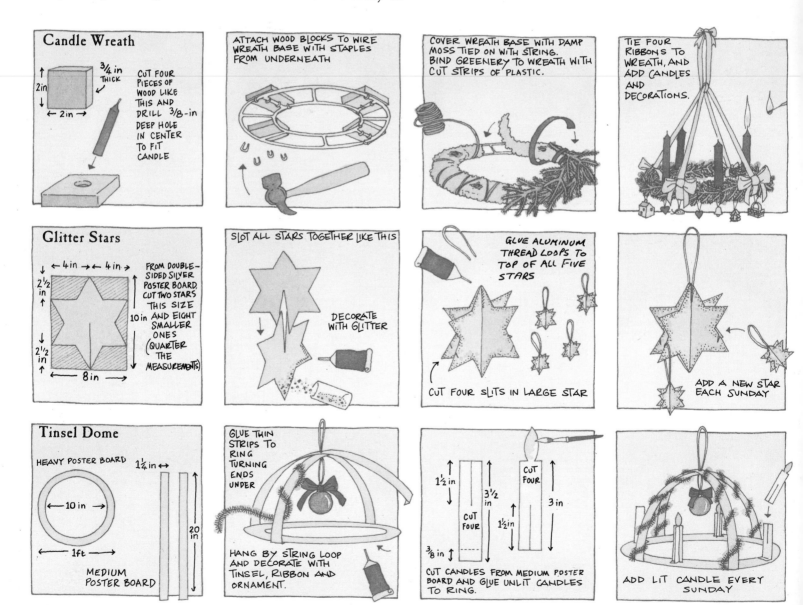

Candle Wreath

2in, 3/4 in THICK, 2in — CUT FOUR PIECES OF WOOD LIKE THIS AND DRILL 3/8-in DEEP HOLE IN CENTER TO FIT CANDLE

ATTACH WOOD BLOCKS TO WIRE WREATH BASE WITH STAPLES FROM UNDERNEATH

COVER WREATH BASE WITH DAMP MOSS TIED ON WITH STRING. BIND GREENERY TO WREATH WITH CUT STRIPS OF PLASTIC.

TIE FOUR RIBBONS TO WREATH, AND ADD CANDLES AND DECORATIONS.

Glitter Stars

4 in, 4 in, 2½ in, 10 in, 2½ in, 8 in — FROM DOUBLE-SIDED SILVER POSTER BOARD, CUT TWO STARS THIS SIZE AND EIGHT SMALLER ONES (QUARTER THE MEASUREMENTS)

SLOT ALL STARS TOGETHER LIKE THIS. DECORATE WITH GLITTER

GLUE ALUMINUM THREAD LOOPS TO TOP OF ALL FIVE STARS. CUT FOUR SLITS IN LARGE STAR

ADD A NEW STAR EACH SUNDAY

Tinsel Dome

HEAVY POSTER BOARD. 1¼ in. 10 in. 1ft. 20 in. MEDIUM POSTER BOARD

GLUE THIN STRIPS TO RING TURNING ENDS UNDER. HANG BY STRING LOOP AND DECORATE WITH TINSEL, RIBBON AND ORNAMENT.

1½ in, 3½ in, CUT FOUR, 1½ in, 3/8 in, CUT FOUR, 3 in. CUT CANDLES FROM MEDIUM POSTER BOARD AND GLUE UNLIT CANDLES TO RING.

ADD LIT CANDLE EVERY SUNDAY

Advent Calendars

Another way to count the days leading up to Christmas is by using an Advent calendar. The type most commonly known is that of a scene, printed on paper, with twenty-four small numbered windows which are opened each day to reveal a picture. Another version is an Advent candle, which is marked in twenty-four sections and lit every day, burning that day's portion. You can easily make your own Advent candle by marking and numbering a thick candle with enamel paint and a fine paintbrush, adding painted stars or holly leaves to decorate. The three calendars shown here can be kept and used each year, with fresh cookies and treats added. Cookie Tree holds twenty-four cookies which have been numbered with frosting, and hung by yarn threaded through a hole made in each cookie before baking; Puzzle Blocks can be made in any size from Christmas card to wall poster; Treat Tree could hold small bath oil pearls, or miniature toys, instead of cookies. . . or a mixture of all three.

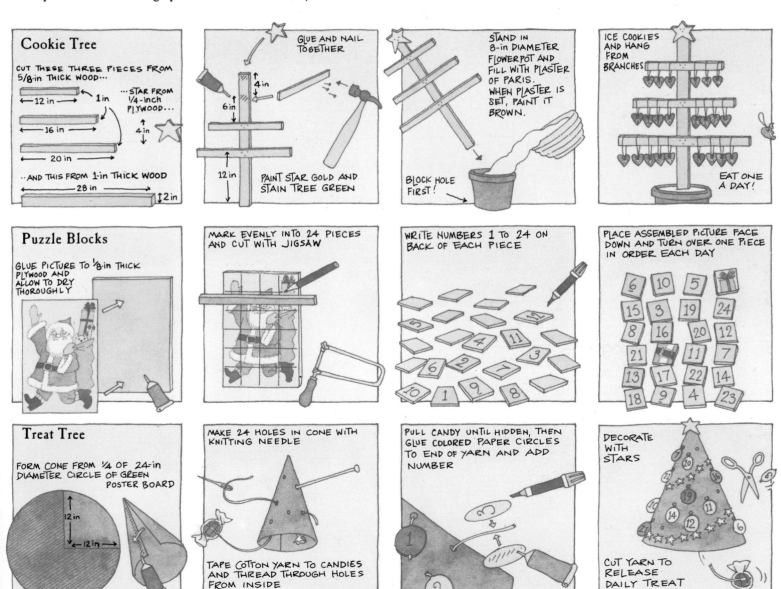

Cookie Tree

CUT THESE THREE PIECES FROM 5/8-in THICK WOOD...

←12 in→ 1 in ...STAR FROM 1/4-inch PLYWOOD...

←16 in→ 4 in

←20 in→

..AND THIS FROM 1-in THICK WOOD
←28 in→ 2 in

GLUE AND NAIL TOGETHER

4 in 6 in 4 in

12 in PAINT STAR GOLD AND STAIN TREE GREEN

STAND IN 8-in DIAMETER FLOWERPOT AND FILL WITH PLASTER OF PARIS. WHEN PLASTER IS SET, PAINT IT BROWN.

BLOCK HOLE FIRST!

ICE COOKIES AND HANG FROM BRANCHES

EAT ONE A DAY!

Puzzle Blocks

GLUE PICTURE TO 1/8-in THICK PLYWOOD AND ALLOW TO DRY THOROUGHLY

MARK EVENLY INTO 24 PIECES AND CUT WITH JIGSAW

WRITE NUMBERS 1 TO 24 ON BACK OF EACH PIECE

PLACE ASSEMBLED PICTURE FACE DOWN AND TURN OVER ONE PIECE IN ORDER EACH DAY

Treat Tree

FORM CONE FROM 1/4 OF 24-in DIAMETER CIRCLE OF GREEN POSTER BOARD

12 in 12 in

MAKE 24 HOLES IN CONE WITH KNITTING NEEDLE

TAPE COTTON YARN TO CANDIES AND THREAD THROUGH HOLES FROM INSIDE

PULL CANDY UNTIL HIDDEN, THEN GLUE COLORED PAPER CIRCLES TO END OF YARN AND ADD NUMBER

DECORATE WITH STARS

CUT YARN TO RELEASE DAILY TREAT

Christmas Cards
Origami Santa Claus

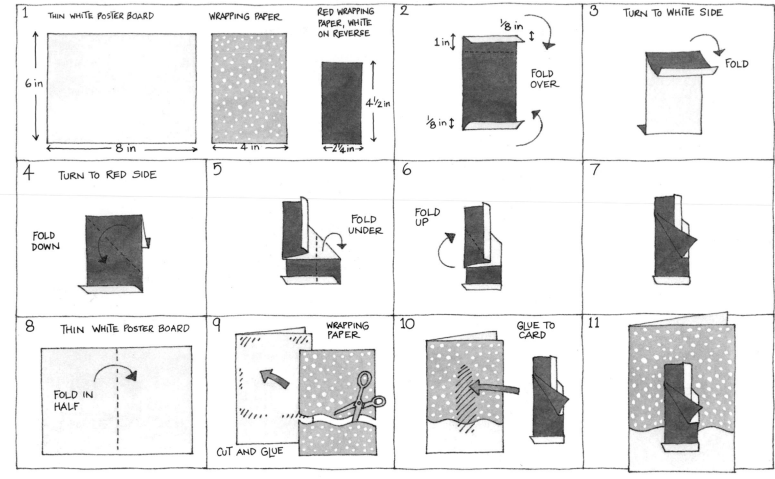

Stained Glass Window

Tissue Paper Christmas Tree

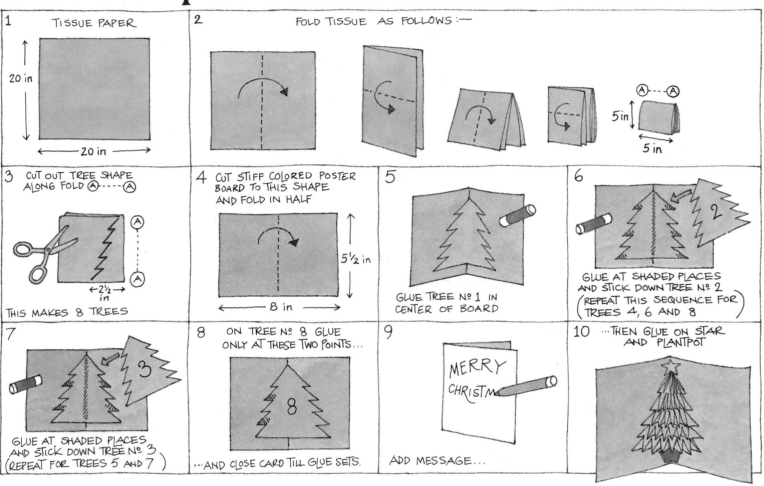

1 TISSUE PAPER
20 in — 20 in

2 FOLD TISSUE AS FOLLOWS:—
5 in — 5 in
(A)···(A)

3 CUT OUT TREE SHAPE ALONG FOLD (A)·····(A)
←2½→ in
THIS MAKES 8 TREES

4 CUT STIFF COLORED POSTER BOARD TO THIS SHAPE AND FOLD IN HALF
5½ in
8 in

5 GLUE TREE №1 IN CENTER OF BOARD

6 GLUE AT SHADED PLACES AND STICK DOWN TREE №2 (REPEAT THIS SEQUENCE FOR TREES 4, 6 AND 8)

7 GLUE AT SHADED PLACES AND STICK DOWN TREE №3 (REPEAT FOR TREES 5 AND 7)

8 ON TREE №8 GLUE ONLY AT THESE TWO POINTS... ...AND CLOSE CARD TILL GLUE SETS.

9 MERRY CHRISTM ADD MESSAGE...

10 ...THEN GLUE ON STAR AND PLANTPOT

Christmas Cracker

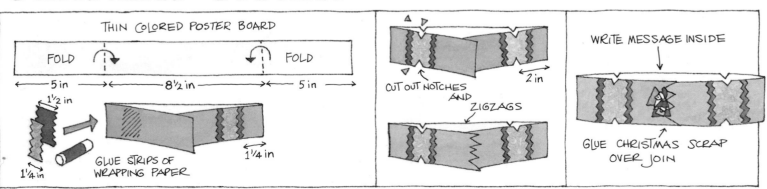

THIN COLORED POSTER BOARD
FOLD   FOLD
5 in — 8½ in — 5 in

1½ in
1¼ in
GLUE STRIPS OF WRAPPING PAPER
1¼ in

CUT OUT NOTCHES AND ZIGZAGS
2 in

WRITE MESSAGE INSIDE
GLUE CHRISTMAS SCRAP OVER JOIN

Handmade Gifts
Grandma Ivy Makes Glove Puppets

HOLLY AND ROBIN HAVE GONE OUT FOR A WALK — SO I'M MAKING THESE FOR THEIR CHRISTMAS PRESENTS

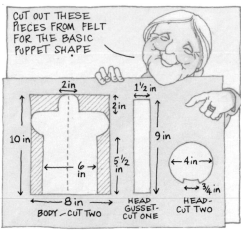

CUT OUT THESE PIECES FROM FELT FOR THE BASIC PUPPET SHAPE

2 in
2 in
1½ in
10 in
9 in
6 in
5½ in
4 in
8 in
BODY — CUT TWO
HEAD GUSSET — CUT ONE
¾ in
HEAD — CUT TWO

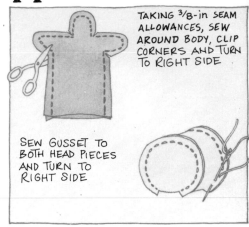

TAKING ⅜-in SEAM ALLOWANCES, SEW AROUND BODY, CLIP CORNERS AND TURN TO RIGHT SIDE

SEW GUSSET TO BOTH HEAD PIECES AND TURN TO RIGHT SIDE

PAD HEAD WITH STUFFING, PUSH NECK INTO HEAD, AND SEW AROUND BASE OF HEAD TO BODY.
NOW COMES THE FUN PART — MAKING DIFFERENT CHARACTERS!

10 in
4 in
BEAD EYES
1½ in → NOSE — GATHER FELT CIRCLE AND STUFF. SEW TO FACE

BEARD AND EYEBROWS FROM BATTING — GLUE TO FACE

EMBROIDER MOUTH

CUT HOOD FROM FELT, FOLD IN HALF AND SEW BACK SEAM. TURN TO RIGHT SIDE. SEW ON POMPOM AND GLUE ON STRIP OF FUR FABRIC. SEW HOOD TO HEAD

GLUE RIBBON BELT AND BUCKLE TO WAIST

← GLUE ON FUR FABRIC STRIPS

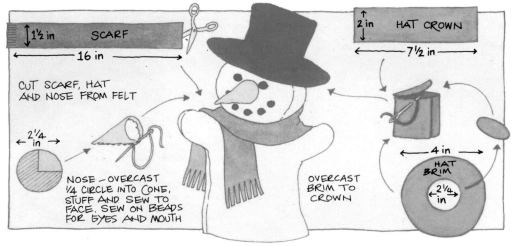

1½ in   SCARF
16 in

CUT SCARF, HAT AND NOSE FROM FELT

2¼ in

NOSE — OVERCAST ¼ CIRCLE INTO CONE, STUFF AND SEW TO FACE. SEW ON BEADS FOR EYES AND MOUTH

2 in   HAT CROWN
7½ in

4 in
HAT BRIM
2¼ in

OVERCAST BRIM TO CROWN

ADD RIBBON AND BELL AT NECK

SEW PIPECLEANER ANTLERS TO HEAD

SEW HEAD TO BODY WITH GUSSET AT FRONT

GLUE ON FELT EARS

BEAD EYES

FELT NOSE

← 2 in

Grandpa Nicholas Makes a Book Stand

CAROL ALWAYS HAS TROUBLE PROPPING UP HER RECIPE BOOKS WHEN SHE'S COOKING — SO HERE'S A PRESENT TO SOLVE THAT!

DRAW PIECES (A) AND (B) ON ⅛-in THICK PLYWOOD AND CUT OUT — I'D USE A JIGSAW FOR PIECE (A)

10 in

1 in

12 in

(A)

(B)

YOU'LL ALSO NEED PIECES (C) AND (D)

2 in

½ in

10 in

(C)

⅜-INCH DIAMETER DOWEL

6 in

(D)

GLUE PIECE (C) TO BASE OF BRANCHES ON PIECE (A)

(A)

(C)

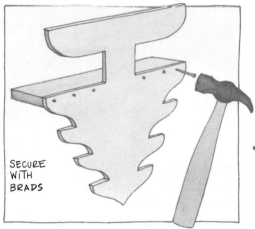

SECURE WITH BRADS

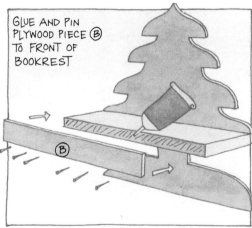

GLUE AND PIN PLYWOOD PIECE (B) TO FRONT OF BOOKREST

(B)

WITH ⅜ in DIAMETER DRILL, MAKE HOLE ½ in DEEP THROUGH BACK INTO BOOKREST. PUSH DOWEL INTO HOLE.

SMOOTH ROUGH EDGES WITH SANDPAPER

DECORATE WITH PAINTED HEARTS AND STARS

PAINT WITH GREEN WOOD STAIN

FINISH WITH COAT OF CLEAR VARNISH

Carol Makes Bow Ties

NOEL DOESN'T OFTEN DRESS UP, BUT WHEN HE DOES HE LIKES TO WEAR A BOW TIE - HERE ARE THREE FOR HIM FOR CHRISTMAS

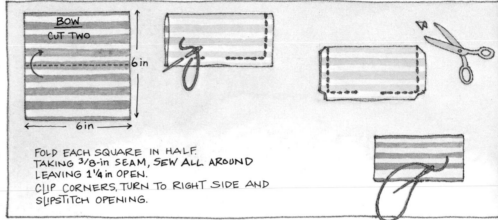

BOW
CUT TWO

6 in

6 in

FOLD EACH SQUARE IN HALF.
TAKING 3/8-in SEAM, SEW ALL AROUND LEAVING 1¼ in OPEN.
CLIP CORNERS, TURN TO RIGHT SIDE AND SLIPSTITCH OPENING.

NECKBAND
CUT ONE

2¼ in

12 in

FOLD IN HALF AND TAKE 3/8 in SEAM ON LONG EDGE AND ACROSS ONE END.

TURN TO RIGHT SIDE AND TURN IN 3/8 in AT OPEN END. SEW PANTS HOOK AT OTHER END.

THREAD 3/8-in METAL RING ONTO 8 in LENGTH OF ¼ in ELASTIC. INSERT IN NECKBAND AND SEW.

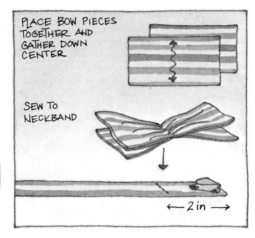

PLACE BOW PIECES TOGETHER AND GATHER DOWN CENTER

SEW TO NECKBAND

← 2 in →

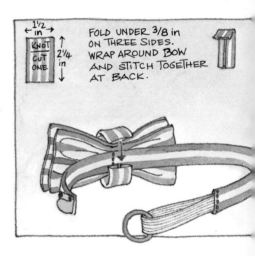

1½ in

KNOT
CUT ONE

2¼ in

FOLD UNDER 3/8 in ON THREE SIDES. WRAP AROUND BOW AND STITCH TOGETHER AT BACK.

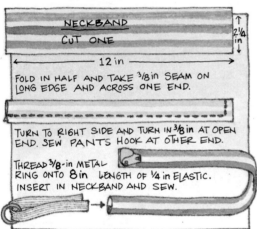

HERE ARE TWO VARIATIONS TO MAKE!

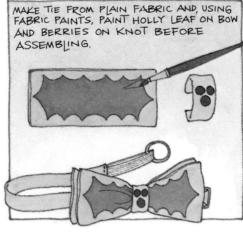

MAKE TIE FROM PLAIN FABRIC AND, USING FABRIC PAINTS, PAINT HOLLY LEAF ON BOW AND BERRIES ON KNOT BEFORE ASSEMBLING.

MAKE TIE FROM RED VELVET. DECORATE WITH STRIPS OF FUR FABRIC. MAKE KNOT FROM BLACK SATIN AND ADD BUCKLE.

Noel Makes a Cheese Box

GRANDPA NICHOLAS LOVES FOOD, SO I'M MAKING THIS CHEESE SAFE FOR HIM. IT'S BIG ENOUGH TO HOLD ALL HIS FAVORITE CHEESES!

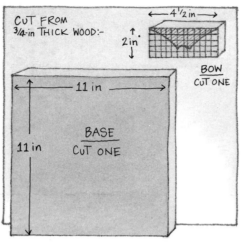

CUT FROM 3/4-in THICK WOOD:-

4 1/2 in

2 in

BOW CUT ONE

11 in

11 in

BASE CUT ONE

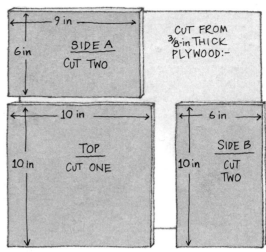

9 in

6 in

SIDE A CUT TWO

CUT FROM 3/8-in THICK PLYWOOD:-

10 in

10 in

TOP CUT ONE

6 in

10 in

SIDE B CUT TWO

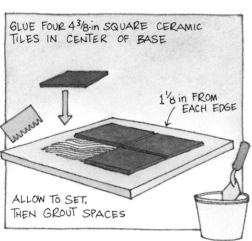

GLUE FOUR 4 3/8-in SQUARE CERAMIC TILES IN CENTER OF BASE

1 1/8 in FROM EACH EDGE

ALLOW TO SET, THEN GROUT SPACES

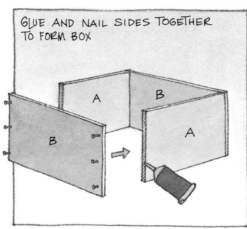

GLUE AND NAIL SIDES TOGETHER TO FORM BOX

A B

B

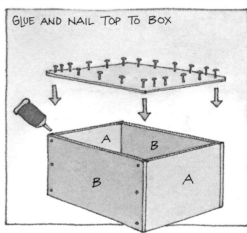

GLUE AND NAIL TOP TO BOX

A B

B A

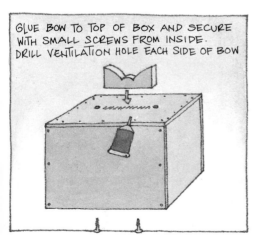

GLUE BOW TO TOP OF BOX AND SECURE WITH SMALL SCREWS FROM INSIDE. DRILL VENTILATION HOLE EACH SIDE OF BOW

SAND EDGES AND PAINT WITH WOOD PRIMER

PAINT WITH ENAMEL PAINT AND DECORATE WITH PAINTED RIBBONS AND MOTIFS.

Holly Makes a Pompom Robin

BABY LIKES PLAYING WITH WOOL POMPOMS, SO I'M MAKING A ROBIN POMPOM FOR CHRISTMAS! FIRST I'LL SHOW YOU HOW TO MAKE A PLAIN ONE.

YOU'LL NEED TWO RINGS OF CARDBOARD AND SOME YARN.

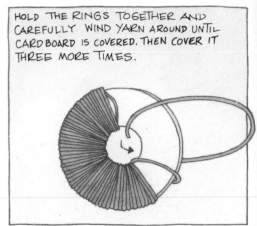

HOLD THE RINGS TOGETHER AND CAREFULLY WIND YARN AROUND UNTIL CARDBOARD IS COVERED. THEN COVER IT THREE MORE TIMES.

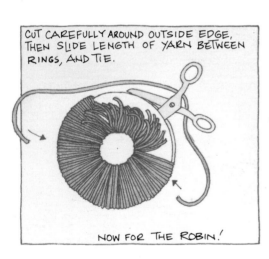

CUT CAREFULLY AROUND OUTSIDE EDGE, THEN SLIDE LENGTH OF YARN BETWEEN RINGS, AND TIE.

NOW FOR THE ROBIN!

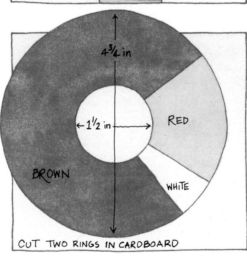

$4\frac{3}{4}$ in

$1\frac{1}{2}$ in   RED

BROWN

WHITE

CUT TWO RINGS IN CARDBOARD

WIND EACH SECTION SEPARATELY — I'VE DONE BROWN AND WHITE, SO FAR — RED'S NEXT!

REPEAT THREE MORE TIMES. CUT AND TIE AS I DEMONSTRATED EARLIER — I HOPE YOU WERE PAYING ATTENTION!

TRIM AWAY UNEVEN ENDS, THEN ADD BEAK, WINGS, TAIL AND EYES CUT FROM FELT (OR BEAD EYES IF FOR AN OLDER CHILD — ME, FOR INSTANCE!)

ON SECOND THOUGHT — PERHAPS BABY WOULD PREFER THE DEMONSTRATION MODEL!

Robin Makes Perfumed Treats

THESE ARE FOR GRANDMA IVY — FIRST TO MAKE IS A SIMMERING SPICE SACK — SHE CAN PUT ONE IN A PAN OF SIMMERING WATER TO SCENT THE WHOLE KITCHEN.

MAKE A SACK FROM FABRIC — CUT IT WITH PINKING SHEARS SO IT DOESN'T FRAY.

← 2 3/4 in →

8 in

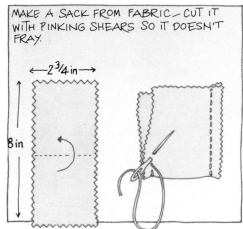

FILL THE SACK WITH :—

BROKEN CINNAMON STICKS

THREE BAY LEAVES

PINCH OF GRATED NUTMEG

SIX CLOVES

DRIED PEEL OF 1/4 ORANGE — BROKEN INTO PIECES

TIE WITH RIBBON

TO MAKE A DRAWER SCENTER — CUT A RECTANGLE OF FABRIC

← 4 3/4 in →

8 in

GLUE INTO TUBE WITH 3/8-in OVERLAP

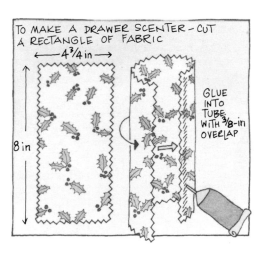

GATHER BOTTOM END. FILL WITH POTPOURRI AND LAVENDER, THEN GATHER OTHER END.

2 in

2 in

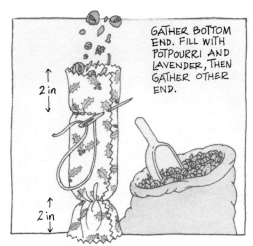

GLUE ON RIBBON AND BOW — GRANDMA CAN PUT THIS BETWEEN THE CLOTHES IN HER DRAWER

NOW FOR A POMANDER — PIN TAPE AROUND ORANGE OR LEMON AND STUD WITH 1 oz OF CLOVES — MAKE HOLES WITH A KNITTING NEEDLE FIRST.

REMOVE TAPE. ROLL POMANDER IN 1 Tbsp. OF ORRIS ROOT POWDER — THIS FIXES THE SCENT. WRAP IN TISSUE AND KEEP IN WARM PLACE FOR THREE WEEKS.

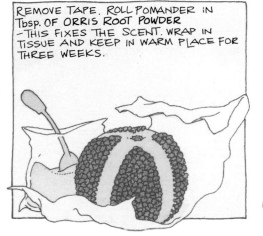

TIE WITH RIBBON AND PLACE WITH THE OTHER TREATS — THEY'LL LOOK NICE IN THIS BASKET I'VE FOUND.

Choosing Presents

Each year we try to find new and exciting Christmas presents for our friends and relatives. A good starting point is to make a list of each person's interests and hobbies, and write down gift ideas that relate to them. Make sure that you buy clothes from a store that will exchange goods if they are the wrong size, or unsuitable. Some items, no matter how useful, can be too personal or boring to rate as presents . . . who wants a corset or cleaning supplies for Christmas? A better idea is to give some little luxury — a special food or perfume — for a treat. It is not always necessary to spend a lot of money on gifts — often a child's drawing, or something handmade, can mean more than a store-bought present. Don't forget that book, garden and gift coupons can be the perfect answer for someone difficult. Below the Tinsel family show their reaction, good and bad, to their gifts.

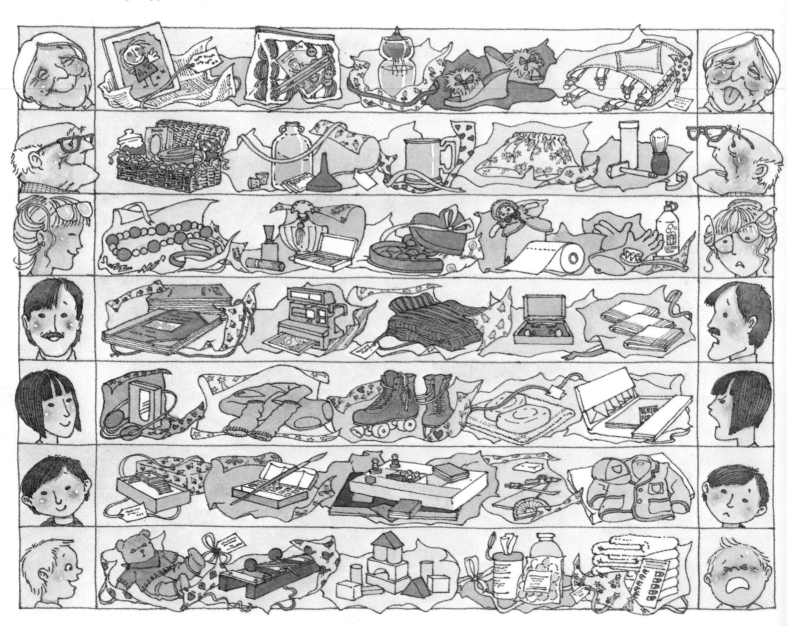

CHAPTER 3

Outside in the Snow

Snowfolk

Snowcastles

LIQUID DETERGENT BOTTLE (WITH TOP AND BOTTOM REMOVED) TO SHAPE TOWERS

TWIG TO MARK WINDOWS

IVY TWINED AROUND TURRET

TWIGS AS STEPS

FIR GARDEN

CARDBOARD BOXES USED TO MOLD SQUARE SHAPES

FUNNEL USED TO SHAPE ROOFS

ICICLES AS DECORATION

Angels in the Snow

Carol Singing

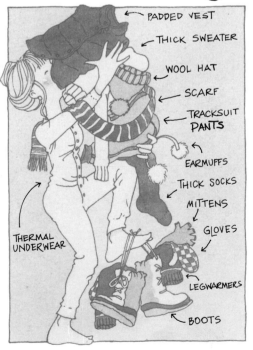

PADDED VEST

THICK SWEATER

WOOL HAT

SCARF

TRACKSUIT PANTS

EARMUFFS

THICK SOCKS

MITTENS

GLOVES

THERMAL UNDERWEAR

LEGWARMERS

BOOTS

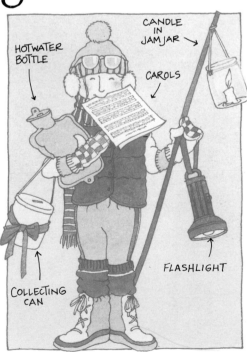

HOTWATER BOTTLE

CANDLE IN JAMJAR

CAROLS

COLLECTING CAN

FLASHLIGHT

HOT COCOA

MINCE PIES

PURSE

Rosemary is a symbol of friendship and remembrance. Said to have become scented when Christ's swaddling cloths were hung over it.

Holly leaves represent Christ's crown of thorns, and the berries, the drops of blood. Guards against the evil eye.

Ivy is said to protect against the effects of drunkenness, and is a symbol of fertility as it refuses to die in winter.

Mistletoe stands for peace, protection and love. An old custom is to kiss under a sprig, picking a berry each time until all are gone.

CHAPTER 4
Yuletide Fashion

Santa Claus Outfit

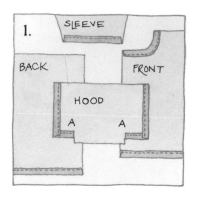

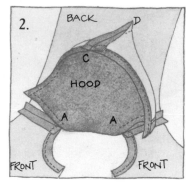

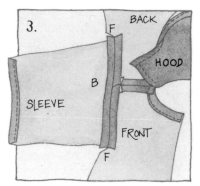

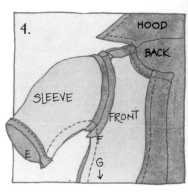

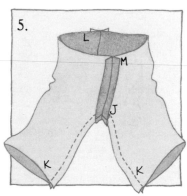

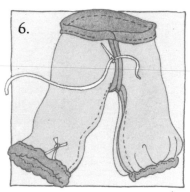

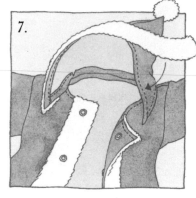

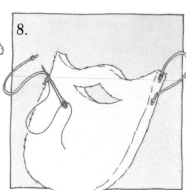

Christmas is Santa's busiest time of the year and he often needs help to hand out all the gifts that he has to deliver. His helpers are allowed to wear this special suit, which can easily be made as follows:

YOU WILL NEED: Red jersey fleece fabric (to find the amount of fabric needed simply lay pattern pieces on the floor within the same measurement as the width of the fabric); 2-inch wide strips of polyester batting, plus a 14 x 10-inch rectangle of batting; ¾-inch-wide elastic to fit around the waist and both legs; 20 inches narrow cord elastic; red sewing thread; fabric glue; five snaps; one white pompom.

TO COMPLETE THE OUTFIT: Black boots; green mittens; black belt with gold buckle; sack.

TO MAKE: ⅝-inch seams taken throughout, with fabric right sides together. Press each seam open after sewing.
1) Turn under ⅝ inch on front neck, sleeve cuffs, front and back jacket hems, and hood (between points C and A), and stitch ⅜ inch from fold.

2) Join shoulder seams AB, then sew hood to back neck along line AA. Join seam CD on hood.

3) Sew sleeves to jacket along line FBF.

4) Join sleeve and side seams, EFG. Turn under 2 inches down jacket fronts and stitch 1½ inches from fold.

5) Join inside leg seams, JK, on each trouser leg. Pin legs together and sew seam LJM around crotch.

6) Turn under 1½ inches at waist and base of legs, and stitch 1⅛ inches in from fold, leaving a space open. Thread each hem with elastic, adjusting to fit. Join elastic and sew across openings.

7) With fabric glue, attach strips of batting to hood and jacket. Position and sew snaps to jacket fronts, overlapping front edges by 2 inches. Sew pompom to point of hood.

8) Sew elastic loops to sides of beard, adjusting to fit, and attach eyebrows to face with eyelash glue.

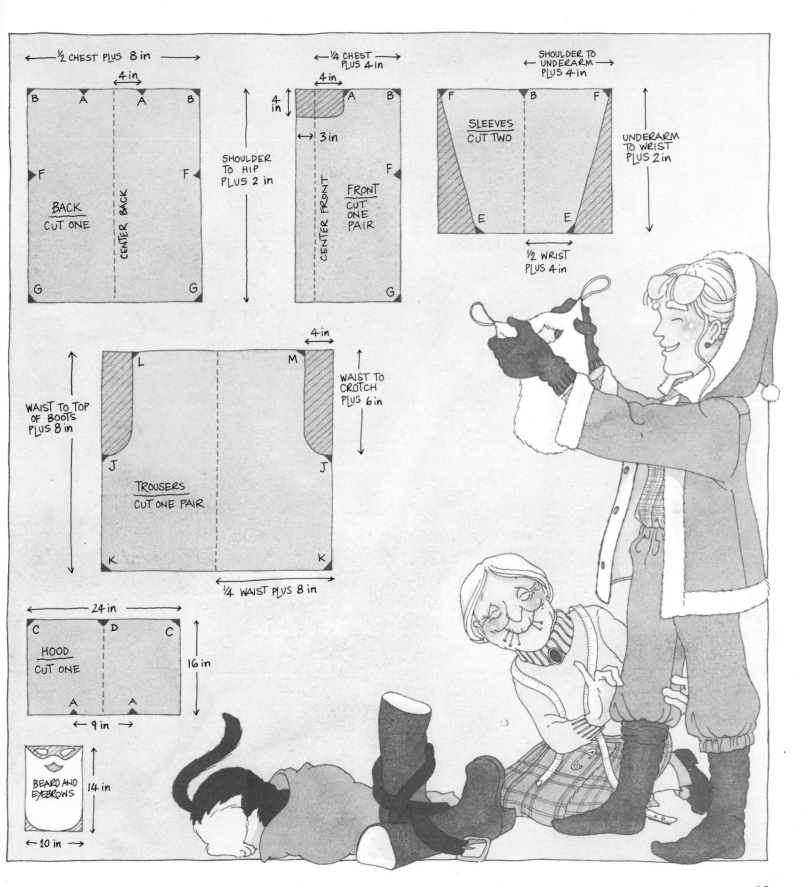

½ CHEST PLUS 8 in

4 in

B   A   A   B

F   F

BACK
CUT ONE

CENTER BACK

G   G

SHOULDER TO HIP PLUS 2 in

¼ CHEST PLUS 4 in

4 in

4 in

A   B

3 in

FRONT
CUT ONE PAIR

CENTER FRONT

F

G

SHOULDER TO UNDERARM PLUS 4 in

F   B   F

SLEEVES
CUT TWO

E   E

½ WRIST PLUS 4 in

UNDERARM TO WRIST PLUS 2 in

4 in

L   M

WAIST TO TOP OF BOOTS PLUS 8 in

J   J

TROUSERS
CUT ONE PAIR

K   K

WAIST TO CROTCH PLUS 6 in

¼ WAIST PLUS 8 in

24 in

C   D   C

HOOD
CUT ONE

A   A

16 in

← 9 in →

BEARD AND EYEBROWS

14 in

← 10 in →

Party Hats

Tiara

THIN POSTER BOARD — 4 in — 12 in

10-in LENGTH OF ELASTIC

GLUE ON WRAPPED CANDIES AS JEWELS

GLUE POSTER BOARD ANTLERS AND EARS ONTO HATBAND

MAKE HALO FROM 24-in MILLINERY WIRE AND COVER WITH TINSEL

CUT AWAY SHADED AREAS. INSERT HALO UNDER FLAP AND GLUE

Cone

POSTER BOARD SEMICIRCLE — 8 in

GLUE INTO CONE SHAPE AND ADD ELASTIC

NET POMPOMS

CREPE PAPER FRILL

GLUE ON PAPER STAR AND CIRCLES

TINSEL

CORK

POSTER BOARD CIRCLE

PAPER BALL

Pillbox

24 in — THIN POSTER BOARD — 4 in

24 in — CREPE PAPER — DEEPER THAN BOARD

GLUE BOARD, OVERLAPPING BY 3/4 in.

GLUE CREPE PAPER TO BOARD

GATHER CREPE PAPER AT CENTER

SECURE WITH STICKER

ELASTIC

FOIL CIRCLE

CREPE PAPER TASSEL

DECORATE WITH STARS AND MOONS

CAKE FRILL

Paper

24 in — CREPE PAPER — 4 in

GLUE TOGETHER, OVERLAPPING BY 3/4 in

WRAPPING PAPER

RIBBON

GLUE PARCELS INSIDE TOP OF 'SACK'

16 in — 24 in

FOLD IN HALF AND GLUE ALONG EDGE

GLUE TRIANGLE ONTO BAND TO MAKE SANTA'S HAT

GLUE TWO CIRCLES TO POINT

CREPE PAPER HOLLY AND SAUCE

CREPE PAPER SEMICIRCLE — 6 in

GLUE PUDDING TO FRONT OF BAND

Christmas Sweaters

To knit

To sew

Christmas Sweaters

Transform your sweaters for Christmas Day by using some of the following ideas.

ABBREVIATIONS: K = knit; P = purl; st(s) = stitch(es); beg = beginning; M = main color; C = contrast color; inc = increase; dec = decrease, cont = continue; g-st = garter stitch; sl = slip: PSSO = pass slipped stitch over; SKTPO = slip 1 stitch, knit 2 together, pass slipped stitch over.

CHRISTMAS CRACKERS

YARN: Remnants of knitting worsted in bright colors and black. NEEDLES: A pair of No.5. TENSION: 22 sts and 30 rows to 4-inch square.

CRACKER: With M cast on 11sts and starting with a K row work even in stockinette st. *Work 6 rows in M. Next row: Keeping yarn not in use at back of work, K 1M, (1C, 3M) twice, 1C, 1M. Next row: P 3C, (1M, 3C) twice. Work 8 rows in C. Next row: K 3C, (1M, 3C) twice. Next row: P 1M, (1C, 3M) twice, 1C, 1M. Work 6 rows in M.* For "pulled" crackers, bind off and work another piece to match. For complete crackers, repeat from * to * once more and bind off.

TO MAKE UP: Darn in ends and press. Gather along center of each stripe worked in C, draw up tightly and secure. Sew crackers to sweater and embroider "snap" lines on "pulled" crackers with a few stitches in black yarn.

CHRISTMAS TREE

YARN: Remnants of 4 ply lurex yarn in silver, gold and mixed colors; a small skein of white 4-ply yarn.

NEEDLES: A pair of No.3.

TENSION: 28 sts and 30 rows to 4-inch square.

ORNAMENTS: With colored lurex cast on 8 sts and starting with a K row work in stockinette st, working random stripes of color. Work 1 row. Cast on 3 sts at beg of next 2 rows. Cast on 2 sts at beg of next 4 rows. Inc 1 st at beg of next 4 rows.

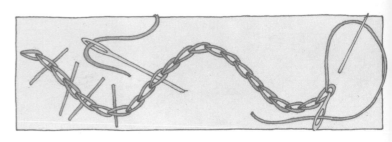

Work 2 rows. Inc 1 st at beg of next 2 rows. Work 8 rows. Dec 1 st at beg of next 2 rows. Work 2 rows. Dec 1 st at beg of next 4 rows. Bind off 2 sts at beg of next 4 rows. Bind off 3 sts at beg of next 2 rows. Work 1 row. Bind off.

CANDLES: With silver cast on 17 sts and starting with a K row work even in stockinette st. Work 2 rows. Bind off 4 sts at beg of next 2 rows (9 sts). Work 6 rows. Change to white and work 26 rows. Bind off 3 sts at beg of next 2 rows (3 sts). Change to gold and work 2 rows. Inc 1 st at beg of next 6 rows (9 sts). Work 2 rows. Dec 1st at beg and end of next 3 rows (3 sts). Next row: P 3 tog, cut yarn and draw through st.

TO MAKE UP: Darn in ends and press. Sew ornaments and candles to sweater: To make "tinsel" embroider lines of chain stitch with silver, then work random stitches through chain.

SNOWMAN

YARN: One 1-oz ball of white mohair; remnants of knitting worsted in red, green and black. PLUS: black wooden beads. NEEDLES: A pair each of No.9 and No.5. TENSION: 17 sts and 22 rows to 4-inch square, with mohair on No.9 needles.

BODY: With No.9 needles and mohair cast on 22 sts and starting with a K row work even in stockinette st. Work 18 rows. Cast on 2 sts at beg of next 4 rows (30 sts). Work 4 rows. Dec 1 st at beg of next 6 rows (24 sts). Dec 1 st at beg and end of next 8 rows (8 sts). Cast on 2 sts at beg of next 2 rows. Inc 1 st at beg of next 2 rows (14 sts). Work 6 rows. Dec 1 at beg of next 2 rows. Dec 1 st at beg and end of next 2 rows (8 sts). Bind off.

HAT: With No.5 needles and black cast on 15 sts and starting with a K row work 18 rows even in stockinette st. Bind off.

SCARF: With red cast on 9 sts and work 6 rows g-st strips of red and green until 54 rows have been worked, bind off. With red cast on 6 sts and work 6 rows g-st stripes of red and green until 24 rows have been worked, bind off.

SNOWFLAKES: With No.9 needles and mohair make a loop and K into front and back of it three times (6 sts). Rows 1, 2, 3, 4 & 5: Sl 1, K5. Row 6: (SKTPO) twice, pass first st over second, break yarn and draw through st.

TO MAKE UP: Darn in ends and press double knitting pieces. Sew snowman to sweater. Sew hat to head and embroider brim in black chain stitch. Sew short scarf piece across neck, and end of long scarf piece to top of neck. Sew snowflakes to sweater, and one to snowman's face for nose. Sew black beads to face for eyes and mouth.

SNOW CRYSTALS

MATERIALS: White yarn and a tapestry needle.

TO MAKE-UP: Work four 2-inch stitches to form a star shape. Where stitches cross secure to sweater with small stitches. Build up snow crystal patterns by working small V-shaped and straight stitches over star.

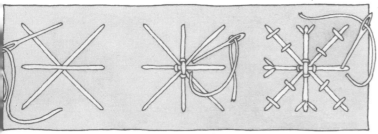

GIFT

MATERIALS: 1½-inch wide satin ribbon to fit around chest of sweater and from shoulder to top of rib on front and back, plus 23½ inches; a 4 x 2-inch rectangle of felt; embroidery cotton; matching sewing threads.

TO MAKE UP: Sew ribbon around chest, overlapping ends at left front. Sew ribbon from top of rib at front to top of rib at back, turning under ½ inch at both ends. Make a bow from remaining ribbon and sew in place. Shape felt to form "tag" and sew in place. Embrioder cord and message on tag with chain stitch.

STARRY NIGHT

MATERIALS: 8 x 4-inch rectangle of black felt; black

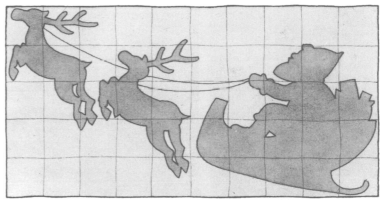

embroidery cotton; small silver star shaped sequins; matching sewing threads.

TO MAKE UP: Following diagram, 1 square represents ¾ inch, cut silhouettes from felt and stitch to sweater. Embroider reins in chain stitch and sew on sequins.

SANTA

MATERIALS: 2-inch wide strips of white fur fabric to fit around base of sweater, sleeve cuffs, and down front of sweater; 1½-inch wide black grosgrain ribbon to fit around sweater plus 4 inches; 8 inches of narrow gold braid; matching sewing threads.

TO MAKE UP: Sew fur fabric in place. Cut end of ribbon to a V and sew around waist, leaving end free. Sew gold braid to "belt" to make buckle.

Festive Jewelery

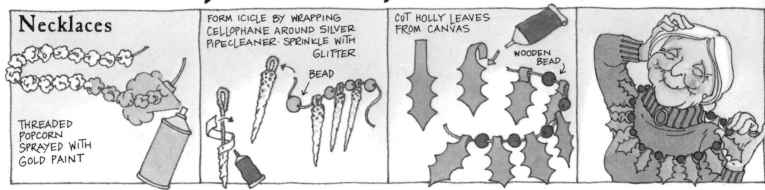

Necklaces

THREADED POPCORN SPRAYED WITH GOLD PAINT

FORM ICICLE BY WRAPPING CELLOPHANE AROUND SILVER PIPECLEANER. SPRINKLE WITH GLITTER

BEAD

CUT HOLLY LEAVES FROM CANVAS

WOODEN BEAD

Bracelets

PLASTIC BANGLE

STRIPES OF TINSEL

STITCH SLEIGH BELLS ONTO LAYERS OF CUT AND STITCHED FELT. TIE WITH RIBBONS

SEW BEADS AND SEQUINS TO HEAVY PACKING CORD FOR FAIRY LIGHT EFFECT

Earrings

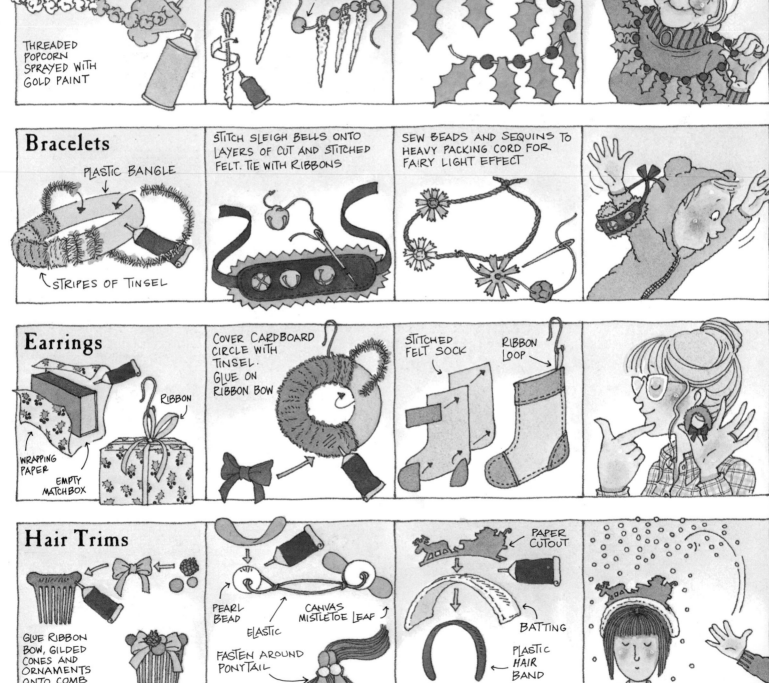

WRAPPING PAPER

EMPTY MATCHBOX

RIBBON

COVER CARDBOARD CIRCLE WITH TINSEL. GLUE ON RIBBON BOW

STITCHED FELT SOCK

RIBBON LOOP

Hair Trims

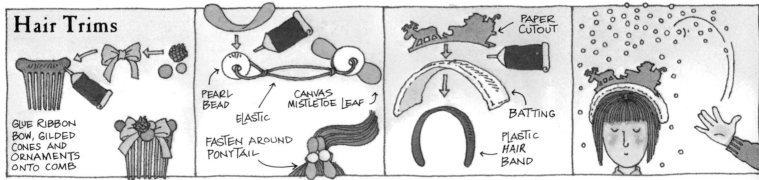

GLUE RIBBON BOW, GILDED CONES AND ORNAMENTS ONTO COMB

PEARL BEAD

ELASTIC

CANVAS MISTLETOE LEAF

FASTEN AROUND PONYTAIL

PAPER CUTOUT

BATTING

PLASTIC HAIR BAND

CHAPTER 5

Decorations and Wrapping

Making Wrapping Paper

Potato Cuts

PUSH A COOKIE CUTTER INTO CENTER OF POTATO HALF— THEN SLICE AWAY 3/8 in AROUND SHAPE

SPREAD POSTER PAINT ONTO SAUCER...

...AND DIP POTATO INTO IT.

PRESS POTATO ONTO PAPER TO MAKE PATTERN...

...ALLOW TO DRY

Stencils

FOLD PAPER IN HALF, CUT OUT SHAPE ALONG FOLD, AND OPEN OUT.

PLACE STENCIL ON PAPER, AND DAB OVER MOTIF WITH SPONGE DIPPED IN PASTE

BEFORE PASTE DRIES, SPRINKLE GLITTER DUST OVER PAPER AND SHAKE OFF ANY EXCESS

Spray Paints

CUT SHAPES FROM THIN PAPER AND DAMPEN WITH A MOIST SPONGE

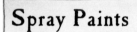

ARRANGE DAMP MOTIFS ON FOIL PAPER

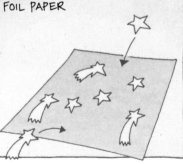

SPRAY STRIPES ACROSS PAPER, USING DIFFERENT COLORS OF SPRAY PAINTS...

...THEN PEEL OFF SHAPES

Marbling

MIX OIL PAINTS WITH TURPENTINE UNTIL RUNNY. POUR ONTO WATER IN STRIPES.

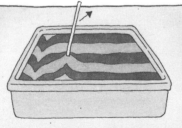

DRAW A STICK ACROSS THE LINES IN ALTERNATE DIRECTIONS.

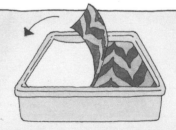

LAY A PIECE OF PAPER ON SURFACE OF WATER, PEEL OFF CAREFULLY AND ALLOW TO DRY

Bows and Trims

Star Bow

CUT SIXTEEN 4¾-IN LENGTHS OF RIBBON. TWIST AND GLUE AS SHOWN.

GLUE TOGETHER IN SETS OF FOUR TO FORM CROSSES.

ASSEMBLE BY GLUEING TOGETHER- PLACING EACH CROSS DIAGONALLY ON TOP OF PREVIOUS CROSS. FINISH WITH LOOP.

Net Pompom

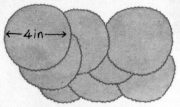

CUT EIGHT 4-in CIRCLES OF NET

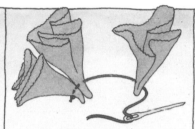

PINCH CENTER OF EACH CIRCLE, CATCH TOGETHER WITH NEEDLE AND THREAD, AND SECURE.

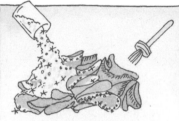

BRUSH EDGES OF NET WITH PASTE AND SPRINKLE WITH GLITTER.

French Swirl

USING NARROW RIBBON, TIE AROUND PACKAGE.

LAY THREE 16-in LENGTHS OF RIBBON ACROSS KNOT AND TIE A BOW

DRAW RIBBON ACROSS SCISSOR BLADE TO FORM RINGLETS

Looped Bow

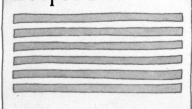

CUT SIX 10-in LENGTHS OF RIBBON

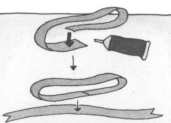

NOTCH BOTH ENDS OF ONE RIBBON, AND GLUE ENDS OF THE OTHERS TO FORM LOOPS. STACK ABOVE EACH OTHER

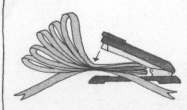

STAPLE THEM ALL TOGETHER AT CENTER...

...AND GLUE BOW TO GIFT

Wrapping Awkward Shapes

Several Small Gifts

DRAW STOCKING SHAPE ON FOLDED FELT, AND SEW ALONG LINE

TRIM TO 3/8 in

PUNCH HOLES AND THREAD WITH RIBBON

To Annie With love from Harry xx

Large and Ungainly

WRAP IN WHITE SHELF LINING PAPER

DECORATE WITH TOY CHRISTMAS TREES AND SKIER

Drum or Tin

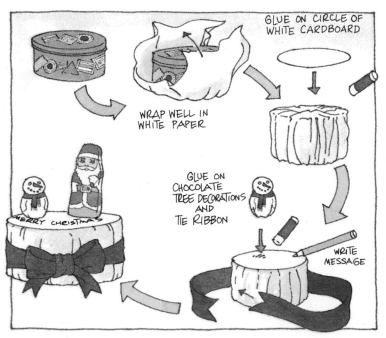

GLUE ON CIRCLE OF WHITE CARDBOARD

WRAP WELL IN WHITE PAPER

GLUE ON CHOCOLATE TREE DECORATIONS AND TIE RIBBON

WRITE MESSAGE

MERRY CHRISTMAS

Bottle or Jar

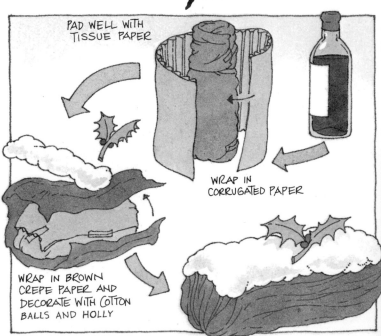

PAD WELL WITH TISSUE PAPER

WRAP IN CORRUGATED PAPER

WRAP IN BROWN CREPE PAPER AND DECORATE WITH COTTON BALLS AND HOLLY

Christmas Crackers

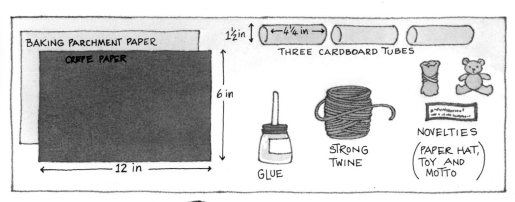

BAKING PARCHMENT PAPER

CREPE PAPER

12 in

6 in

1½ in

4¼ in

THREE CARDBOARD TUBES

GLUE

STRONG TWINE

NOVELTIES
(PAPER HAT, TOY AND MOTTO)

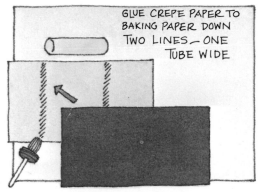

GLUE CREPE PAPER TO BAKING PAPER DOWN TWO LINES—ONE TUBE WIDE

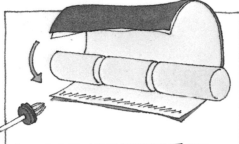

ROLL PAPER AROUND THREE TUBES PLACED END TO END, AND SECURE WITH GLUE

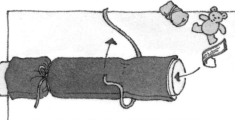

PLACE NOVELTIES INSIDE MIDDLE TUBE; WIND TWINE AROUND CRACKER WHERE TUBES MEET. PULL TIGHTLY AND KNOT

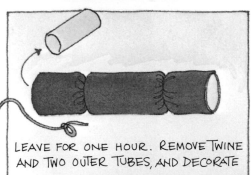

LEAVE FOR ONE HOUR. REMOVE TWINE AND TWO OUTER TUBES, AND DECORATE

SPOTTY PAPER

CUTOUT FIGURE

DOILIES

FRINGED ENDS

RIBBON BOW

PAPER INITIAL

PAINTED CONES

NET BOW

SERRATED EDGES

SEQUINS

Wreaths, Garlands and Logs

Cornucopia Wreath

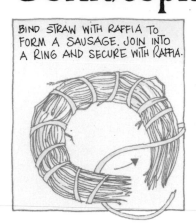

BIND STRAW WITH RAFFIA TO FORM A SAUSAGE. JOIN INTO A RING AND SECURE WITH RAFFIA.

TAKE SMALL BUNCHES OF GREENERY AND BIND ONTO WREATH WITH GREEN STRING.

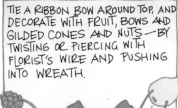

TIE A RIBBON BOW AROUND TOP, AND DECORATE WITH FRUIT, BOWS AND GILDED CONES AND NUTS — BY TWISTING OR PIERCING WITH FLORIST'S WIRE AND PUSHING INTO WREATH.

Greenery Garland

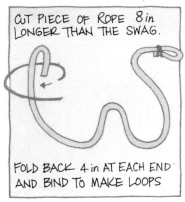

CUT PIECE OF ROPE 8in LONGER THAN THE SWAG.

FOLD BACK 4in AT EACH END AND BIND TO MAKE LOOPS

BIND BUNCHES OF FOLIAGE TO ROPE WITH STRING, KEEPING BUNCHES LYING IN ONE DIRECTION

SLIP A CURTAIN RING ON TO RIBBON AND TIE A BOW AT EACH LOOPING POINT.

Yule Log

DRILL HOLES IN LOG TO HOLD CANDLES

MIX SOAP POWDER WITH WATER TO FORM A THICK PASTE AND WHIP UNTIL FROTHY.

NAIL EVERGREENS TO LOG, THEN DECORATE WITH SOAP SNOW, AND ORNAMENTS.

Garlands and Chains

Folded Fans

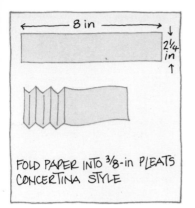

FOLD PAPER INTO ⅜-in PLEATS CONCERTINA STYLE

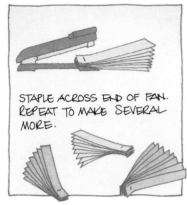

STAPLE ACROSS END OF FAN. REPEAT TO MAKE SEVERAL MORE.

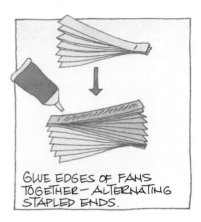

GLUE EDGES OF FANS TOGETHER—ALTERNATING STAPLED ENDS.

Twisting Spiral Chain

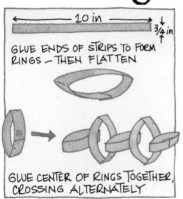

GLUE ENDS OF STRIPS TO FORM RINGS—THEN FLATTEN

GLUE CENTER OF RINGS TOGETHER, CROSSING ALTERNATELY

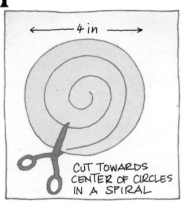

CUT TOWARDS CENTER OF CIRCLES IN A SPIRAL

THREAD SPIRAL TO EACH ALTERNATE RING, SECURING WITH A KNOT AT EACH END

Tissue Stars

CUT TWO 6-POINTED STARS FROM CARDBOARD, AND A PILE OF STARS FROM FOLDED TISSUE PAPER

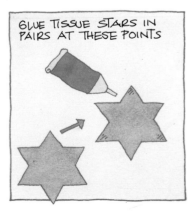

GLUE TISSUE STARS IN PAIRS AT THESE POINTS

WHEN DRY, GLUE PAIRS OF STARS TOGETHER AT THESE POINTS—THEN GLUE A CARDBOARD STAR AT EACH END OF GARLAND

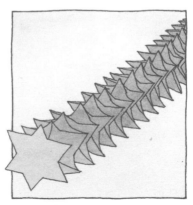

Box Theatre

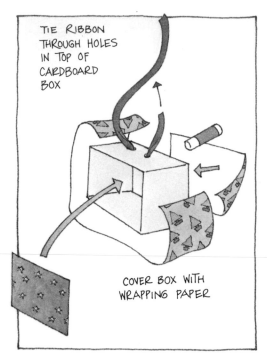

TIE RIBBON THROUGH HOLES IN TOP OF CARDBOARD BOX

COVER BOX WITH WRAPPING PAPER

DECORATE AS YOU WISH (GLITTER, COTTON, ETC.)

CUT FIGURES FROM CHRISTMAS CARDS AND GLUE INSIDE BOX

Snow Scene

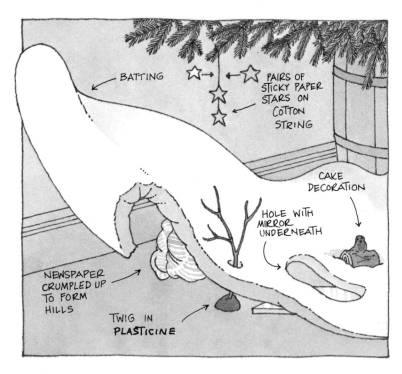

BATTING

PAIRS OF STICKY PAPER STARS ON COTTON STRING

CAKE DECORATION

HOLE WITH MIRROR UNDERNEATH

NEWSPAPER CRUMPLED UP TO FORM HILLS

TWIG IN **PLASTICINE**

CHAPTER 6

The Christmas Tree

Types of Christmas Tree

Blocked Tree

Cut Tree

Imitation Tree

Rooted Tree

Looking After Christmas Trees

Any bare spaces can be filled by pushing spare branches, trimmed from base of tree, into holes drilled in trunk.

Cut trees drop their needles quickly due to moisture loss. Spraying daily with lukewarm water helps prevent this.

Soak the roots of bare rooted trees overnight in water, then pot the tree in moist soil. Place away from direct heat.

Cut 2-in from base of trunk and wedge in bucket or tub with stones and crumpled newspapers. Keep container filled with water daily.

If space is limited, prune back of tree to a flat shape and place against a wall. Use cut branches to make wreaths and garlands.

Victorian Tree

SUSPEND BIRD DECORATION BY NYLON THREAD STITCHED TO BACK

PIN RIBBON TO BEAK

LACE

¼ CIRCLE OF NET

4 in

← PIPE CLEANER

FILL WITH POTPOURRI AND TIE WITH RIBBON

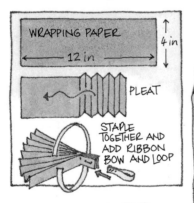

WRAPPING PAPER

4 in

12 in

PLEAT

STAPLE TOGETHER AND ADD RIBBON BOW AND LOOP

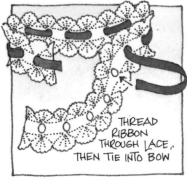

THREAD RIBBON THROUGH LACE, THEN TIE INTO BOW

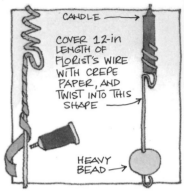

CANDLE

COVER 12-in LENGTH OF FLORIST'S WIRE WITH CREPE PAPER, AND TWIST INTO THIS SHAPE

HEAVY BEAD →

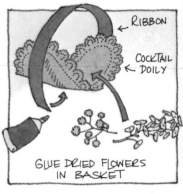

← RIBBON

COCKTAIL DOILY

GLUE DRIED FLOWERS IN BASKET

CORK →

CARD →

CRAFT STICK

CLOTHES PIN →

↑ GOLD RIBBON

6 in SQUARE OF POSTER BOARD

CURL INTO CONE SHAPE AND GLUE

PUNCH HOLE AND THREAD WITH RIBBON

GLUE ON ZIGZAG BRAID

FILL WITH CANDIES

Child's Own Tree

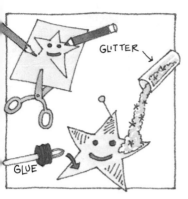

GLITTER

GLUE

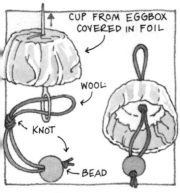

CUP FROM EGGBOX COVERED IN FOIL

WOOL

KNOT

BEAD

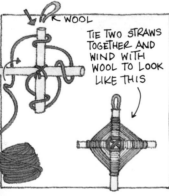

WOOL

TIE TWO STRAWS TOGETHER AND WIND WITH WOOL TO LOOK LIKE THIS

DOUGH = ONE CUP FLOUR AND ONE CUP SALT MIXED WITH WATER

ROLL OUT AND CUT INTO SHAPES

HOLE FOR RIBBON

HARDEN IN SLOW OVEN, THEN PAINT

WRAPPING PAPER

8 in

4 in

RIBBON

1¼ in

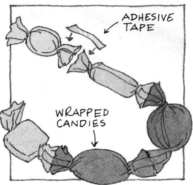

ADHESIVE TAPE

WRAPPED CANDIES

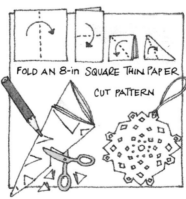

FOLD AN 8-IN SQUARE THIN PAPER

CUT PATTERN

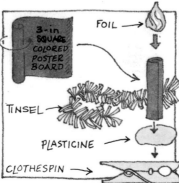

3-in SQUARE COLORED POSTER BOARD

FOIL

TINSEL

PLASTICINE

CLOTHESPIN

Food Lover's Tree

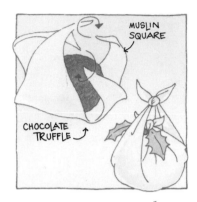

MUSLIN SQUARE

CHOCOLATE TRUFFLE

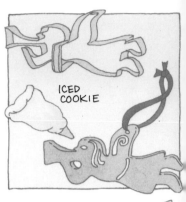

ICED COOKIE

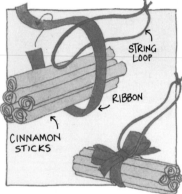

STRING LOOP

RIBBON

CINNAMON STICKS

POPPING CORN (TO COVER BASE OF PAN)

1 TABLESPOON HOT OIL

FORM INITIALS FROM BREAD DOUGH STRIPS

BRUSH WITH BEATEN EGG

SPRINKLE WITH SEEDS OR NUTS, AND BAKE

FILL CHRISTMAS CRACKER WITH FAVORITE COFFEE BEANS

NET RECTANGLE SEWN TO MAKE SACK

FILL WITH NUTS AND TIE WITH RIBBON

CARVE SPIRAL CHANNEL IN LEMON OR ORANGE

STUD WITH CLOVES

HANG UP WITH STRING LOOP

Wildlife Tree

PEANUT

ROSEHIP

STRING

CUT SHAPES FROM BREAD AND DRY IN SLOW OVEN

SPREAD PINECONE WITH PEANUT BUTTER, AND DIP INTO BIRDSEED

MELTED FAT AND SEEDS

LEAVE TO SET

HOT SKEWER

BEAD

STRING

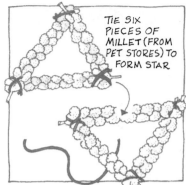

TIE SIX PIECES OF MILLET (FROM PET STORES) TO FORM STAR

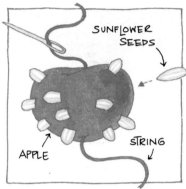

SUNFLOWER SEEDS

APPLE

STRING

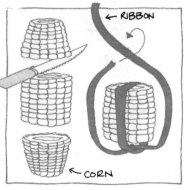

RIBBON

CORN

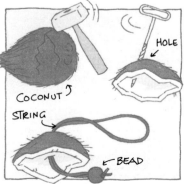

COCONUT

STRING

HOLE

BEAD

49

Soft and Safe Tree

FELT

STUFF WITH KAPOK

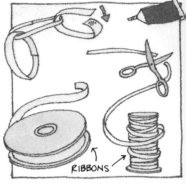

RIBBONS

COTTON BALLS

FABRIC

RIBBON

FELT ¼ CIRCLE

PAPER BALL

STRANDS OF WOOL TIED WITH PIPE CLEANERS

GLUE TOGETHER

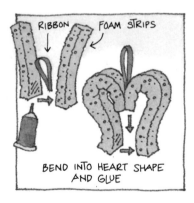

RIBBON   FOAM STRIPS

BEND INTO HEART SHAPE AND GLUE

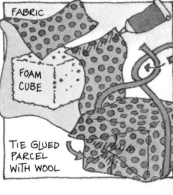

FOAM CUBE

TIE GLUED PARCEL WITH WOOL

TWO CARDBOARD CIRCLES

WIND WITH COLORED WOOLS TO COVER FOUR TIMES.

CUT, TIE AND NEATEN

PAPER STAR

RIBBON

GATHERED NET SKIRT

CHAPTER 7

Santa Claus

Writing to Santa Claus

Humility – It is always better to let Santa decide whether you deserve to have a visit from him, rather than take it for granted.

Flattery – Everybody likes to be flattered, and Santa is no exception. Let him know how much you look forward to his visits.

Bribery – The way to Santa's heart is to mention that you intend to leave him some food and a warming drink if he should call.

Advice – Because Santa has so many people to choose presents for, it helps if you can give him some idea of what you would like.

Politeness – Always remember to say "please" and "thank you" to show Santa how well-behaved and considerate you are.

Dear Santa Claus,

If you decide that I have been good enough this year for you to bring me some gifts, I promise to leave some tasty treats for you by the fireplace.

Should you be wondering what to give me, please may I suggest that expensive presents are a good idea, as they always go up in value.

I would love to meet you some day because you look very handsome on all our Christmas cards.

Thank you very much for sparing the time to read this letter.

With lots of love,

Holly

xxx

From Letter to Sack

After your letter to Santa Claus has been written and mailed (or left somewhere to be collected), a lot happens before you receive your gifts. Here you can see how your request is taken to be processed in the elf workshop's, making sure that the correct presents are placed in Santa's sack ready to be delivered to you.

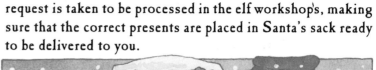

53

Yule Lodge

Santa Claus lives in a quaint wooden house built high among the trees, which might even be in a forest near to your home. This is where all your letters are delivered, and where the elves spend many busy weeks leading up to Christmas making and wrapping presents in their workshops. Santa's reindeer have their stables attached to the house, and as Christmas approaches they are given extra helpings of moss and hay to make them strong enough to pull the gift-laden sleigh. Afterwards they all return here to have a well-earned rest.

Food to Leave for Santa

Hard candies for Santa to suck if he starts to feel air sick, and extra strong peppermints to keep him warm on a frosty night.

Decorate mince pies with stars cut from left-over pastry. Dust with powdered sugar and pile on a plate with a chunk of cake.

Roll and cut bread dough into a tree shape and snip surface with scissors, Bake and serve with sharp cheese and crunchy pickles.

Don't forget the reindeers! Leave them a bundle of sweet meadow hay, a bunch of reindeer moss and a crisp red apple.

Leave a jug of hot cocoa with a shaker of chocolate and cinnamon, and a bowl of punch in case Santa feels like something stronger.

Chimneys

Although some chimneys are narrow, with the help of a rope, Santa can deliver your gifts to your home anyway.

Mesh guards, to stop birds nesting, can prove to be difficult to remove and replace if Santa has forgotten his tool kit.

A cowl on a chimney-top is tricky to squeeze through, although it does stop snow falling onto Santa's head once he is in the chimney.

A wide-necked chimney-pot with a rounded edge is easy to get down, and good foot-holds can be found in brick or stone stacks.

A chimney-pot with a pointed edge is extremely uncomfort-able to get down, and could catch Santa's beard or tear his clothes.

The Busiest Time of the Year

CHAPTER 8

F estive Fare

Figgy Pudding

DRIED FIGS

BUTTER

MOLASSES

BAKING POWDER

MILK

EGGS

CINNAMON

GRATED NUTMEG

ALL-PURPOSE FLOUR

DARK BROWN SUGAR

POWDERED SUGAR

GRATED LEMON RIND

CREAM

HOLLY

FRESH WHITE BREADCRUMBS

IF YOU HAVEN'T MADE THE CHRISTMAS PUDDING BY STIR-UP SUNDAY (THE LAST SUNDAY BEFORE ADVENT) HERE'S A RECIPE FOR ONE THAT DOESN'T NEED TO MATURE.

CUT STEMS FROM 9 OZ DRIED FIGS WITH KITCHEN SCISSORS, THEN CUT FIGS INTO SMALL PIECES. THIS IS VERY STICKY, SO BE WARNED!

SIMMER THE FIGS IN 2/3 CUP MILK FOR 25 MINUTES, REMOVE FROM HEAT AND STIR IN 2 TABLESPOONS MOLASSES

MIX TOGETHER IN BOWL:
1 GENEROUS CUP FLOUR,
1/2 CUP PACKED BROWN SUGAR,
1 1/3 CUP BREADCRUMBS,
1 TEASPOON EACH OF BAKING POWDER, CINNAMON AND NUTMEG, AND THE GRATED RIND OF 1 LEMON. THEN ADD FIG MIXTURE, 7 TBSP MELTED BUTTER, AND 2 BEATEN EGGS.
MIX WELL.

BUTTER A 1-QT PUDDING MOLD AND SPOON IN MIXTURE

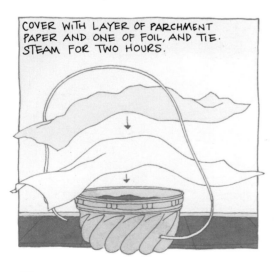

COVER WITH LAYER OF PARCHMENT PAPER AND ONE OF FOIL, AND TIE. STEAM FOR TWO HOURS.

TURN OUT ONTO A PLATE, DUST WITH POWDERED SUGAR AND DECORATE WITH SPRIG OF HOLLY. SERVE WITH WHIPPED CREAM.

I DON'T NORMALLY GIVE THIS RECIPE AWAY, BUT YOU'RE SPECIAL!

Warming Punches

ALCOHOLIC PUNCH:-

ORANGES   CLOVES   GRATED NUTMEG

LIGHT BROWN SUGAR

RED WINE   CINNAMON STICKS

CUT AN ORANGE INTO 4 PIECES AND PUSH 3 CLOVES INTO EACH PIECE

MIX TOGETHER 1 BOTTLE RED WINE (I'M USING A MIXTURE OF MY HOMEMADE ELDERBERRY AND BLACKBERRY), 1 CUP SUGAR, AND ½ TEASPOON GRATED NUTMEG

POUR INTO A LARGE SAUCEPAN (DON'T USE ALUMINUM OR ENAMEL AS THEY REACT WITH THE ALCOHOL — DON'T WE ALL!) WITH THE ORANGE PIECES AND GENTLY HEAT UNTIL ALMOST BOILING

STRAIN INTO A PUNCH BOWL AND FLOAT SLICES OF ORANGE ON TOP

SERVE IN MUGS WITH A CINNAMON STICK

NON-ALCOHOLIC PUNCH:-

GINGER ALE

UNSWEETENED APPLE JUICE   UNSWEETENED PINEAPPLE JUICE

CINNAMON

APPLE

LEMON JUICE   SUGAR CUBES

RUB 3 SUGAR CUBES OVER SURFACE OF A LEMON UNTIL THEY TURN YELLOW. MIX TOGETHER WITH 2½ CUPS APPLE JUICE, 2 CUPS PINEAPPLE JUICE, 1¼ CUPS GINGER ALE, 1 TEASPOON LEMON JUICE AND ½ TEASPOON CINNAMON. STIR UNTIL SUGAR IS DISSOLVED.

HEAT UNTIL ALMOST BOILING AND POUR INTO GLASSES DECORATED WITH APPLE SLICES.

Savory Chestnut Log

DRIED CHESTNUTS
ONION
GARLIC
VEGETABLE STOCK CUBE
EGGS
MIXED HERBS
SALT
CELERY
PUFF PASTRY
BLACK PEPPER
VEGETABLE OIL
ALL-PURPOSE FLOUR
GROUND ALMONDS
CHESTNUT PUREE
BREADCRUMBS
WHITE WINE

SOAK 3½oz DRIED CHESTNUTS OVERNIGHT IN COLD WATER. SIMMER IN FRESH WATER FOR 30 MINUTES, DRAIN AND CHOP

SAUTÉ 1 CHOPPED ONION AND 2 CRUSHED CLOVES OF GARLIC IN 2 TABLESPOONS OIL UNTIL SOFT

STIR IN 2 TABLESPOONS FLOUR, THEN ADD ½ CUP WINE, ¼ CUP WATER, AND CRUMBLED STOCK CUBE. STIR UNTIL THICK AND REMOVE FROM HEAT

STIR IN 2 BEATEN EGGS, 9 oz CANNED CHESTNUT PUREE, AND ⅔ CUP DRY BREADCRUMBS

ADD 2 STALKS FINELY DICED CELERY, CHOPPED CHESTNUTS, 2 TEASPOONS MIXED HERBS, 1 TEASPOON SALT AND BLACK PEPPER TO TASTE — MMM!

ROLL AND TRIM 18 oz PUFF PASTRY TO 12-in SQUARE.

PLACE MIXTURE DOWN CENTER OF PASTRY AND PINCH EDGES TOGETHER. CUT TRIMMINGS INTO THIN STRIPS, WIND INTO 2 SPIRALS AND FIT IN EACH END OF LOG.

PLACE ON GREASED BAKING TRAY, BRUSH WITH BEATEN EGG AND BAKE FOR 1 HOUR AT 375°F.

SPRINKLE WITH GROUND ALMONDS AND ADD ROBIN DECORATION

Spiced Nuts

SAVORY ALMONDS:—

VEGETABLE OIL · SOY SAUCE · TABASCO · SALT · PAPRIKA · EGG

SESAME SEEDS · SHELLED ALMONDS

MIX TOGETHER 1 TABLESPOON EACH OF OIL, SOY SAUCE AND SESAME SEEDS, 1 EGG WHITE AND A DASH OF TABASCO. ADD 4 OZ SHELLED ALMONDS AND STIR UNTIL NUTS ARE COATED

SPREAD ON A COOKIE SHEET AND BAKE AT 275°F FOR 15 MINUTES, TURNING NUTS SO THEY ROAST EVENLY

MIX TOGETHER 1 TEASPOON EACH OF SALT AND PAPRIKA, AND ROLL NUTS IN MIXTURE WHILE STILL HOT. LEAVE TO COOL

SWEET WALNUTS OR PECANS:—

BROWN SUGAR · CORNSTARCH · CINNAMON

ALLSPICE · EGG

GRATED NUTMEG · WALNUTS OR PECANS

MIX TOGETHER ¼ CUP SUGAR, 2 TBSP CORNSTARCH, 1½ TEASPOONS CINNAMON, AND ½ TEASPOON EACH OF ALLSPICE AND NUTMEG

BEAT TOGETHER 1 EGG WHITE AND 1 TABLESPOON WATER. TIP 4 OZ NUTS INTO EGG MIXTURE AND STIR TO COAT

DROP NUTS SINGLY INTO DRY INGREDIENTS, TURN UNTIL COVERED, THEN PLACE ON GREASED BAKING TRAY

BAKE FOR 1 HOUR AT 275°F, TURNING ONCE DURING COOKING. LEAVE TO COOL. THEY'RE GREAT TO NIBBLE DURING CHRISTMAS!

Christmas Pudding Truffles

POWDERED SUGAR

BUTTER

VANILLA EXTRACT

COCOA

CHOCOLATE SPRINKLES

ARTIFICIAL HOLLY

WHIPPING CREAM

CAKE

IN A BOWL, CREAM TOGETHER 4 TBSP BUTTER, 1 CUP POWDERED SUGAR, 4½ TBSP COCOA...

...2 TABLESPOONS WHIPPING CREAM, AND ½ TEASPOON VANILLA EXTRACT — EXCUSE ME WHILE I JUST CONCENTRATE

ADD 3 CUPS CAKE CRUMBS AND MIX WELL — WE CAN HAVE THE REST OF THE CAKE FOR TEA

ROLL INTO BALLS ABOUT THE SIZE OF A WALNUT — I HAPPEN TO HAVE ONE HERE TO HELP YOU

ROLL EACH BALL IN CHOCOLATE SPRINKLES TO COVER — I LIKE TO KEEP A STORE OF THESE AS I HAVE A SWEET TOOTH

MIX ½ CUP POWDERED SUGAR WITH 1 TEASPOON HOT WATER AND DROP A SMALL AMOUNT ONTO THE TOP OF EACH TRUFFLE — THIS NEEDS A STEADY HAND!

DECORATE WITH TINY SPRIGS OF ARTIFICIAL HOLLY

THIS ACTUALLY MAKES 16 TRUFFLES, BUT AS THERE ARE 7 IN OUR FAMILY, IT SAVES ARGUMENTS IF I EAT 2 NOW — THEN IT'S JUST 2 EACH!

Cream Cheese Snowmen

WHITE BREADCRUMBS

CREAM CHEESE

SHREDDED COCONUT

SALT

CHOPPED MIXED NUTS

CARROTS

TOOTHPICKS

MEASURE 2 CUPS FRESH WHITE BREADCRUMBS, 1 CUP CHOPPED MIXED NUTS, AND 9 oz CREAM CHEESE INTO A BOWL TOGETHER WITH A PINCH OF SALT AND MIX WELL

DIVIDE MIXTURE INTO 2 PIECES, ONE TWICE THE SIZE OF THE OTHER, AND ROLL 12 BALLS FROM EACH PORTION

ROLL EACH BALL IN SHREDDED COCONUT TO COVER—THIS IS A BIT MESSY

MAKE HAT FROM PEELED CARROT BY CUTTING A 5/8-in LENGTH FROM POINTED END, AND A THIN SLICE FROM THE THICK END

I'M ALLOWED TO USE A KNIFE IF AN ADULT WATCHES ME— SO YOU BE CAREFUL TOO!

PUSH A TOOTHPICK THROUGH CARROT PIECES, THEN THROUGH HEAD AND BODY OF SNOWMAN

MARK EYES, MOUTH AND BUTTONS WITH A TOOTHPICK...

...AND INSERT A SLIVER OF CARROT FOR NOSE

THIS MAKES 12 SNOWMEN AND THEY'RE REALLY TASTY!

Chocolates and Candies

CHOCOLATE CREAMS :-

POWDERED SUGAR

EGG

SEMISWEET CHOCOLATE

FLAVORING EXTRACTS

FOOD COLORING

MIX TOGETHER 2 CUPS POWERED SUGAR AND 1 LIGHTLY BEATEN EGG WHITE AND KNEAD UNTIL SMOOTH

DIVIDE INTO 3 PORTIONS, THEN ADD A FEW DROPS OF COLORING AND FLAVORING TO EACH PIECE AND KNEAD UNTIL EVENLY COLORED

VIOLET EXTRACT + MAUVE COLOR =

ROSE EXTRACT + PINK COLOR =

PEPPERMINT EXTRACT + GREEN COLOR =

ROLL EACH PIECE TO 2in THICK, CUT INTO SHAPES, PLACE ON FOIL AND LET DRY OVERNIGHT

MELT 8oz CHOCOLATE AND DIP IN EACH CANDY TO COAT HALF. LEAVE ON FOIL TO SET

WITH THE REMAINING CHOCOLATE I'LL MAKE SOME NUT CLUSTERS - MIX 6oz MIXED NUTS AND 2oz RAISINS WITH THE CHOCOLATE. DROP SMALL SPOONFULS ONTO FOIL AND LEAVE TO SET

STUFFED DATES :-

MARZIPAN

DATES

SUPERFINE SUGAR

DIVIDE A 4-oz BLOCK OF MARZIPAN INTO 20 PIECES AND ROLL EACH INTO A SAUSAGE SHAPE

REMOVE PITS FROM 20 DATES, PLACE MARZIPAN INSIDE EACH DATE AND ROLL IN SUPERFINE SUGAR

CHAPTER 9
Christmas Fun and Games

Charades

The game of charades involves one person acting out the name of a song, television program, book film or play without making any sound, while the other people try to guess the mime. Begin by holding up the same number of fingers as there are words, then mime the words in turn. The actions shown below will be of some help.

SONG: Open mouth and arms, as in singing.

TELEVISION: Draw square shape in front of you.

BOOK: Open hands like the pages of a book.

FILM: Pretend to wind an old movie camera.

PLAY: Draw two curves like opening curtains.

THE WHOLE THING: Draw a circle in front of you.

SOUNDS LIKE: Tug your ear lobe.

SIMILAR: Rock clenched hands to and fro.

SHORTER OR LONGER: Move hands closer or apart.

SMALL WORD: Pretend to hold tiny word.

PROPER NAME: Pat top of head with hand.

SYLLABLES: On upper arm indicate with fingers.

Charades can be played in three ways. 1. The first player thinks up a mime, and the one who guesses it correctly takes over. 2. Two teams choose their own subjects, and a member from one team mimes to the other team in turn. 3. The titles are written on pieces of paper by someone who is not playing, and are drawn in turn from a hat.

Pass the Present

With paper taken from the Christmas presents, wrap a small gift to make a large parcel. One person whistles, the players sit in a circle, and the parcel is passed around clockwise. When the music stops, the person holding the parcel begins to open it, but must pass it on as the music starts. The winner is the one who unwraps the gift.

Build a Snowman

The object of this game is to be the first person to complete a drawing of a snowman by throwing a die. The correct number must be thrown before each part of the snowman can be drawn in this order: body (6); head (5); hat (4); scarf (3); three buttons (2 for each); eyes, then nose, and then mouth (1 for each).

Pin the Star on the Tree

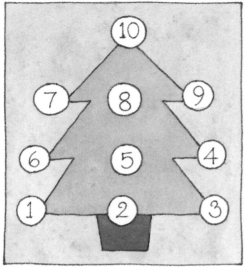

Copy the Christmas tree shown in the diagram onto a large sheet of paper, and pin to a wall. Cut a star from gold paper and push a thumbtack through it. Blindfold one player, turn them round three times, then ask them to pin the star on top of the tree. Count up everybody's scores, and the highest number wins.

Popcorn Chain

Divide players into two teams, get them to stand in line, and give each person a drinking straw. Place a bowl of popcorn at one end of each line, and an empty bowl at the other end. The object is to get the most pieces of popcorn into the empty bowls in 2 minutes, passing it between players by sucking it up with the straws.

Snowball!

Two teams of players sit at a table and a cotton wool ball is given to one team. These players pass the ball between them, under the table, then place their fists on the table. A member of the other team guesses which hand holds the ball and touches it, shouting "SNOWBALL!" The ball is passed to that team if the guess is correct.

Blow out the Candles

Cut ⅜-inch tabs around the base of a cardboard tube and bend outwards. Glue to a 3-inch circle of cardboard and glue a cardboard flame to top of tube. Make nine more candles and paint. Place in the formation shown, and stand 10 feet away. Take turns to roll a soft ball at the candles, and keep a score of how many you knock over. The highest number wins.

Fill Santa's Sack

Open a large brown paper bag and place on the floor. Divide a pack of colored cotton balls into even groups of pink, yellow, blue and white. Four players choose a color each, stand with their backs 2 yards from the bag, and throw the balls over their shoulders. Count the number of balls each player gets into Santa's sack.

Musical Christmas Crackers

On a table place one less cracker than there are players. When the music starts the players walk clockwise around the table, and as the music stops everyone grabs a cracker. The person without one drops out of the game, and one cracker is removed. Continue until one cracker, remains, which is given to the player holding it.

Christmas Tree Lights Game

Up to four players each choose a color. Start at the plug, and move counters along the lights by throwing a die. If you land on a Santa bulb, go on to the next bulb in your color. If you land on a clear bulb, go back to the last bulb in your color. Landing on an empty socket sends you back to the start. First to reach the star wins.

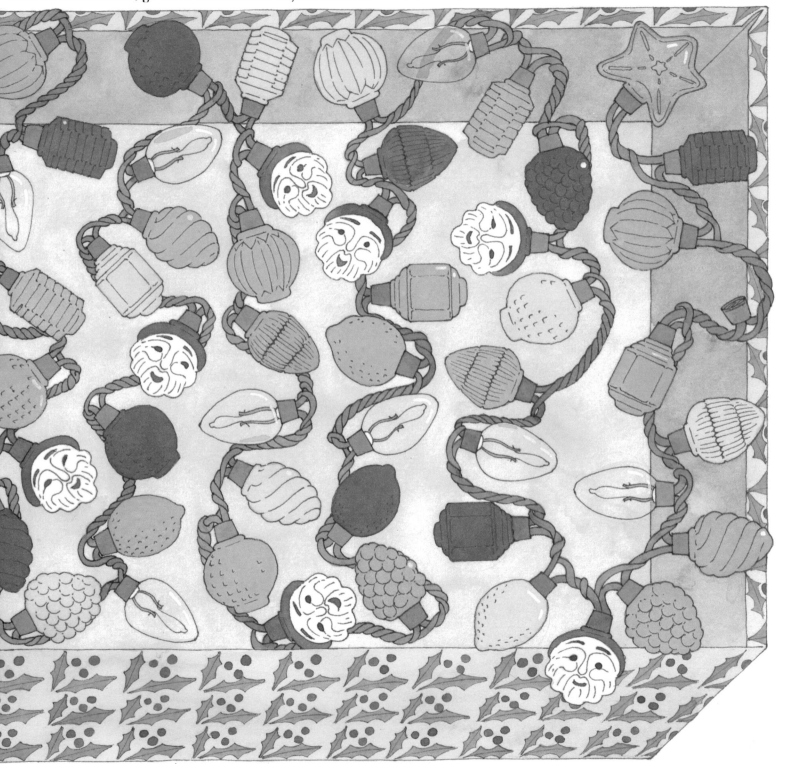

75

Puzzles and Tricks
Sleeping Snowbaby

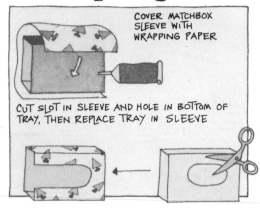

COVER MATCHBOX SLEEVE WITH WRAPPING PAPER

CUT SLOT IN SLEEVE AND HOLE IN BOTTOM OF TRAY, THEN REPLACE TRAY IN SLEEVE

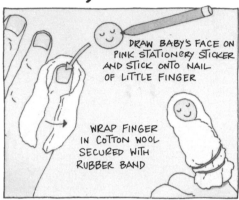

DRAW BABY'S FACE ON PINK STATIONERY STICKER AND STICK ONTO NAIL OF LITTLE FINGER

WRAP FINGER IN COTTON WOOL SECURED WITH RUBBER BAND

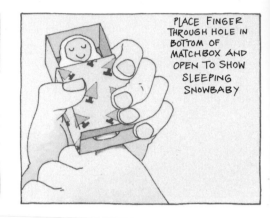

PLACE FINGER THROUGH HOLE IN BOTTOM OF MATCHBOX AND OPEN TO SHOW SLEEPING SNOWBABY

Spinning Medallion

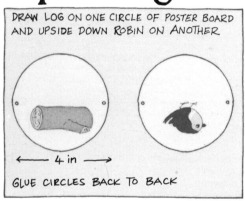

DRAW LOG ON ONE CIRCLE OF POSTER BOARD AND UPSIDE DOWN ROBIN ON ANOTHER

← 4 in →

GLUE CIRCLES BACK TO BACK

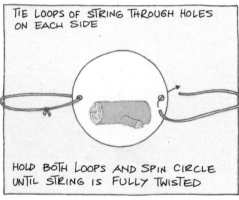

TIE LOOPS OF STRING THROUGH HOLES ON EACH SIDE

HOLD BOTH LOOPS AND SPIN CIRCLE UNTIL STRING IS FULLY TWISTED

AS CIRCLE SPINS, THE ROBIN WILL APPEAR TO BE STANDING ON LOG

Mirror Drawing

DRAW HOLLY ON INDEX CARD

GLUE ONE MATCHBOX TO BACK OF SMALL MIRROR...

.. AND ANOTHER TO BLANK INDEX CARD

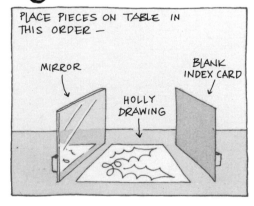

PLACE PIECES ON TABLE IN THIS ORDER —

MIRROR

HOLLY DRAWING

BLANK INDEX CARD

TRY TO TRACE AROUND HOLLY WHILE LOOKING IN MIRROR

Gnome Visitor

CURTAINS OVER DOORWAY

WEAR COAT BACK TO FRONT AND BUTTONED AT NECK

BEARD

TABLE COVERED WITH CLOTH

Go Back, Rudolph!

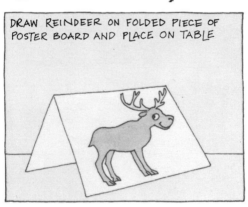

DRAW REINDEER ON FOLDED PIECE OF POSTER BOARD AND PLACE ON TABLE

RUDOLPH HAS LEFT THE SLEIGH BEHIND— HOW CAN YOU MAKE HIM GO BACK WITHOUT TOUCHING THE CARD?

PLACE A FULL GLASS OF WATER IN FRONT OF CARD 2 in AWAY. WITH EYES LEVEL WITH GLASS, LOOK AT CARD. RUDOLPH HAS CHANGED DIRECTION

Tie the Parcel

CAN ANYONE TIE THE RIBBON ROUND THE PARCEL WITHOUT LETTING GO OF THE ENDS?

I SIMPLY FOLD MY ARMS, PICK UP THE RIBBON...

... AND THEN UNFOLD MY ARMS!

Rescue Baby!

Here is a game for one player. You have to rescue Baby, who has become entangled with paper chains. First throw a die to see which member of the family is going to help you, and start at the number you have thrown. Follow the chain carefully to try and reach Baby in the Middle, then return along the chain to your starting point.

CHAPTER 10

After Christmas

Keeping in Touch

The lull after Christmas, and before the celebrations of New Year, is ideal for writing to, or telephoning, friends and relations to thank them for gifts – and also an opportunity to renew old friendships. Many people visit relatives who were unable to join them for the holidays, maybe taking some leftover treats to share.

"Thank You"

Visiting Relatives

New Year

Just before midnight on December 31st the front door and windows are opened to let out the old year and let in the new.

People also make resolutions to improve themselves in the coming year. It is a time for beginning anew.

First Footing

Resolutions

It's Better to Give . . .

CHAPTER 11

Christmas Around the World

Sweden

In Sweden the celebrations last for a month – from Saint Lucia's Day on December 13th to Saint Knut's Day on January 13th. On Saint Lucia's Day, Swedish families are awakened with coffee and freshly baked buns by the daughter of the house. She is dressed in a white gown with a red sash, and wears on her head a wreath of greenery topped with lighted candles. Often she is joined by "Star Boys," who wear pointed hats and carry star wands. To end the Christmas meal "rice porridge" is served. This is rice pudding containing a single almond . . . the person who finds the nut will marry within the next year!

Denmark

A traditional Danish Christmas tree decoration is a woven, heart-shaped paper basket, which is filled with candies. Other decorations are made from carved wood, woven and plaited straw, and colored paper. The tree is topped with a shining star, and lit by candles. Each Sunday in Advent, guests are invited to join in the lighting of the candles on the Advent crown. Adults drink a warming mixture of red wine, spices and raisins, and children drink a sweet fruit juice, such as strawberry. Everybody eats small cakes of batter which have been cooked over the fire in a special pan, and dusted with powdered sugar.

Finland

In Finland everybody's house is given a thorough cleaning in readiness for Christmas. In the kitchen, hours are spent cooking and baking special treats for the festive season. Before Christmas Eve many people make a traditional visit to the famous Finnish steam baths. Fir trees are felled, tied onto sleds, and taken home to be decorated. Often a sheaf of grain is tied to a pole, together with nuts and seeds, and placed outside in the garden as a Christmas treat for the birds. It is said that many peasants will refuse to eat their Christmas meal until their feathered friends have been fed.

Norway

Norwegian children always remember a little gnome called "Nisse" at Christmastime. He guards all the farm animals, and he plays tricks on the children if they forget to put out a bowl of special porridge for him. A favorite holiday cookie called "sand kager" is made by mixing together 2 cups each of butter and sugar, 4 cups of flour, and 1 cup of chopped almonds. This is pressed into pan, baked until golden brown, and cut into squares. In the dark afternoons the Viking tradition of "Christmas buck" is practiced by children, dressed in outlandish outfits, who go from house to house asking for goodies.

Germany

In Germany Christmas preparations begin on the eve of December 6th. People often set aside special evenings for baking spiced cakes and cookies, and making gifts and decorations. Little dolls of fruit are traditional Christmas toys. They are easily made by forming a figure from plastic-covered wire and threading with raisins, apple slices, and nuts. Children leave letters on their window sills for Christkind, a winged figure dressed in white robes and a golden crown, who distributes gifts. Sometimes these letters are decorated with glue and sprinkled with sugar to make them sparkle.

Austria

The feast of Saint Nicholas marks the beginning of Christmas in Austria. The saint, accompanied by the devil, asks children for a list of their good and bad deeds. Good children are given candies, toys and nuts. Gifts, which have been placed under the tree, are opened after dinner on Christmas Eve. Austrian wax tree decorations can be made by pouring melted beeswax into cookie or chocolate molds, pushing a yarn loop into the wax, and leaving them to set. Brass instruments play chorale music from church steeples, and carol singers, carrying blazing torches and a manger from house to house, gather on the church steps.

Switzerland

As Christmas approaches, Swiss children eagerly await the tinkling of a silver bell that heralds the arrival of Christkindli – a white-clad angel, with a face veil held in place by a jeweled crown. The tree candles are lit as she enters each house and hands out presents from the basket held by her child helpers. The week before Christmas children dress up and visit homes for small gifts. Bell ringing has become a tradition, and each village competes with the next when calling people to midnight Mass. After the service, families gather to share huge homemade doughnuts called "ringli" and hot chocolate.

France

In France, on Christmas Eve, children leave their shoes by the fireplace to be filled with gifts by Père Noël. In the morning they also find that candies, fruit, nuts and small toys have been hung on the tree. In cathedral squares the story of Christ's birth is re-enacted by both players and puppets. In addition to the usual Biblical characters, many cribs include painted clay figures called "santons," which represent people of everyday life, such as the priest, mayor, policeman, baker or grocer. These can be made from modeling clay and painted when hard, and added to your own crib.

Italy

The Italian festive season starts eight days before Christmas, and continues until Epiphany. A strict fast is observed for twenty-four hours before Christmas Eve, and is followed by a celebration meal, in which a light Milanese cake called "panettone" features. Presents, and sometimes empty boxes, are drawn from the "Urn of Fate" – a grab bag that always contains one gift per person. By twilight, candles are lighted around the family crib, prayers are said, and children recite poems. Befana, a kindly witch, arrives on January 6th and leaves gifts for good children, and a piece of charcoal for bad ones.

Spain

In Spain the Christmas festivities begin on 8th December, the Feast of the Immaculate Conception, when the Dance of the Sixes is performed. As in cathedrals and churches, most homes have a manger scene, complete with carved figures. During the week before Christmas, families gather round their manger to sing, while children play tambourines and dance. Shoes are placed on balconies on the night of 6th January, in the hope that the Wise Men will fill them with gifts. Often bundles of straw are also left for the camels. You could place a large foil star in your window to attract the Wise Men.

Australia

Christmas comes in the middle of the Australian summer, when the weather is very hot. After exchanging gifts at the breakfast table, many people have their Christmas Day meal on the beach, followed by a celebration supper. Homes are decorated with ferns and palm leaves, together with special flowers. One, called the Christmas bush, consists of hazy clusters of tiny flowers; another, the Christmas bell, is a bell-shaped flower with a yellow edge. A potted palm could be decorated to become a Christmas tree. As evening falls, parks fill with hundreds of people for carol services by candlelight.

Mexico

The Mexican home must be decorated, and ready to receive guests, by December 16th — the beginning of "Posadas," which commemorates Mary and Joseph's search for lodgings. Homes are festooned with Spanish moss, evergreens and colored lanterns and a crib is erected in the corner of one room. After prayers, fireworks are lit, and people gather to break the "Pinata" — an earthenware jar filled with treats, which is hung from the ceiling. Blindfolded children try to break it with a stick to release the contents. Simple Pinatas can be easily made by covering inflated balloons with papier mâché.

United States

Christmas celebrations vary greatly among regions of the United States, as the inhabitants are of many ethnic origins. In Pennsylvania, the Moravians build a landscape – called a "Putz" – under the Christmas tree; while the Germans are given gifts by Belsnickle, who taps them with his switch if they have misbehaved. In the South, firearms are shot to greet distant neighbors on Christmas Day. In Alaska a star on a pole is taken from door to door, followed by "Herod's men," who try to capture the star. Colonial doorways are often decorated with a pineapple, a symbol of hospitality.

Canada

Christmas is observed in Canada in very much the same manner as in northern parts of the United States – but also in other ways in some of its provinces: a big midwinter festival –called Sinck tuck– is celebrated by the Eskimos, with dancing and a present-giving party; in Labrador, turnips are saved from the summer harvest and are given to children, with a lighted candle pushed into a hollowed-out hole; and in Nova Scotia, a country settled by Scottish highlanders, songs and carols, brought from Brittany and the Basque country two centuries ago, are sung each Christmas morning.

CHAPTER 12

Twelfth Night

Taking Down Decorations

Twelfth Night, or Epiphany, falls on the 6th January, and marks the end of the Christmas holidays. After this date it is considered unlucky to still have decorations in the house, so we take them down, to be packed away safely until next Christmas. Greenery is taken outside and either planted in the garden or thrown away.

Half fill a jar with pine needles, add 1 teaspoon of vodka, and top up with corn oil. Shake daily for 1 week, strain and use as bath oil.

Iron large pieces of undamaged used wrapping paper and roll around a cardboard tube. Keep to wrap next year's gifts.

Small glass ornaments can be packed in egg cartons. Larger decorations should be wrapped in tissue and packed between foam.

Tighten light bulbs, and wrap cord around a piece of cardboard. Pack in a box, with a layer of cotton on each side for protection.

Greeting cards can be made into gift tags by cutting into rectangles, circles or triangles with pinking shears and adding yarn ties.

Useful Tips About Greenery

Keep a small piece of holly until next Christmas for good luck. Burn all other dead greenery, and use the ashes as a garden fertilizer.

Sprays of ivy, arranged in water with cut flowers, may have grown small roots by now. These can be put in a planter.

Remove dead greenery from the wreath. If the frame is metal, rub with steel wool and a little oil to prevent rusting, and pack away.

If your Christmas tree has roots, dig a hole in the garden, fork in some peat and firm the soil round the tree's roots. Water well.

A Christmas Collage

An unusual way to remember a special Christmas is to make a collage, using photographs, scraps of wrapping paper, gift tags, greeting cards, feathers and nuts gathered on walks, cracker scraps, paper hats, and pretty wrappers from candies and chocolates eaten over the holidays. Every collage will be unique – just like every Christmas.

Index